T0103226

GOD
MADE
YOU

YOU!

GLENN HASCALL

GOD MADE YOU YOU!

DEVOTIONS FOR BOYS

BARBOUR **kidz**

A Division of Barbour Publishing

© 2024 by Barbour Publishing, Inc.

ISBN 978-1-63609-925-5

Published by Barbour Publishing, Inc., 1810 Barbour Drive, Uhrichsville, Ohio 44683, www.barbourbooks.com

Our mission is to inspire the world with the life-changing message of the Bible.

Printed in China.

002127 0824 HA

INTRODUCTION

Who you are at this moment is not who you will be one day. The steps you take today will either lead you closer to or further away from God's best. That's what this book is all about.

The you that includes a heart, soul, and mind is being reshaped by God. He's not standing by to remind you of all the things you've done wrong. God is standing by to help you do good things in a great way.

God knows your thoughts and plans. He understands your emotions too. He recognizes that there's fear hiding somewhere inside, and He wants to send it away. God made you with a plan and purpose that's bigger than any struggle you face. He'll never leave you and never deny knowing you.

Turn each page and come face-to-face with the God who can take you just as you are and make you someone exceptional. There's no need to give up if it seems hard because the God who created you is right here—right now. And He's ready to speak to your heart, if you are listening.

YOU'RE WONDERFUL

God wanted good to come to them.
GENESIS 1:28

Some people think God made humans and then made life hard for them on purpose. They think God doesn't really care about people very much. They see bad things happen and believe God had something to do with it. *He didn't.*

God spoke the world into existence. He made animals, fish, plants, and planets. He made air to breathe, water to drink, and food to eat. After He made each of these things, God said the work so far was "good." He said something different after He made humans. At that point, God said creation was "very good" (Genesis 1:31).

Why would God make things hard for people that He said were more important to Him than anything else He created? *He wouldn't.*

You need to know, and should always remember, that God thinks you're wonderful—and He wants good to come to you.

. . . .

Thank You for making me, God. Help me remember that You love me and want good things for me. Grow my trust in You.

7

A GREAT LOVE

God showed His love to us.
ROMANS 5:8

God takes care of everything—*everything.* The rotation of planets? His idea. Using bats to control mosquitoes? God did that. The ingredients for your favorite treat? Yep, God. As much as He made all good things, the only creation He's ever said He *loves* is humans. He loves you. Everything He made was something you can enjoy. He did that for you— because He loves you.

When you break His rules, He loves you enough to make sure you have a way to be forgiven: Jesus. Yesterday, you read that everything God made was "good," but after He made humans, He said creation was "very good." The Bible says God loves people—those who do right and those who do not. The rest of today's verse says, "While we were still sinners, Christ died for us." He loves *all* people. Every single one.

If His greatest love is for you, then you should love God more than anyone else.

. . . .

When I say I love video games, sports, or music, I'm saying something different than what You said, Father. It's amazing to know that You love me more than the things I do or enjoy.

HONORABLE CHOICES

All things are made for Him.
May He be honored forever.
ROMANS 11:36

God made you *you*—on purpose, with big plans for your life because He loves you. He didn't make a mistake when He made you, so you never have a reason to think you're a mistake. Sure, you can *make* mistakes, but you can never *be* a mistake.

You might pay attention to the way you look or a physical challenge you live with. You might think God would like you more if you could make more friends. You might even think you need to be something you're not. But from the day you were born, God never believed it was a good idea to change who He created you to be.

Some people make choices they think will make them happier. God made you and wants you to make choices that honor Him. Instead of simple happiness that can come and go, God offers joy when you make honorable choices—and that joy lasts forever.

Lord, I want to honor You because You made me.
I want to make choices that prove I trust you.

BEING FOUND

You are good and ready to forgive, O Lord.
You are rich in loving-kindness to all who call to You.
PSALM 86:5

You might not always expect God's kindness, but He is always ready to offer it to you. Boys sometimes make choices that break God's rules. You have. The Bible said you would. Romans 3:23 says, "All. . .have sinned." That doesn't leave anyone out.

God didn't create you to break His rules, but He knew you would. He also knew that people who break His rules want to hide from Him. They're afraid they'll be in trouble, but God doesn't work like that. His kindness keeps bringing boys like you back to God.

You enjoy kindness, and kindness is something you can share with others. It should be part of the *you* God made you to be. The kindness God shows you can help you make friends with boys who used to be enemies. It can help those who are hiding to enjoy being found.

. . . .

I need to remember that You're kind, God. When I want to hide after I have sinned, help me remember that You want to forgive me and show kindness that can help keep me close to You.

IN THE DETAILS

All the days of my life were written in [God's]
book before any of them came to be.
PSALM 139:16

Experts say there are no two fingerprints that are exactly
the same. The same is supposedly true for snowflakes.
Likewise, nobody on earth is exactly like you.

God's never been confused about who you are, what
you'll do, or why He's willing to help you.

You're not someone that God can't figure out. He made
you and knew all about you before you were born. He
knew what you would do yesterday and today. And God
even knows all this information about every single person
who's ever lived.

Even knowing all the bad things that people will do, God
chose to love more than anyone could hate. God knows
every sin you'll ever commit and still makes the choice to
love you from the beginning. He doesn't stop.

. . . .

You made me one-of-a-kind, Father.
I'm here because You gave me life and
purpose. Now please give me the courage
to watch Your plan come true.

ADOPTION APPROVED

*He gave the right and the power to become
children of God to those who received Him.
He gave this to those who put their trust in His name.*
JOHN 1:12

God's plan has always been that you would choose to
become one of His children. He offers everything you need
to become His son. This process is called adoption, and it
requires your willingness to be brought into God's family.

If you need strength to believe in Him, then God can
give you that. Over the next few days, you'll read about
character traits God wants to build in your life. Those traits
can be learned when God becomes your spiritual Father.

On your own, the best you can do is to do better, be
nicer, and try harder. Change is hard when you try to do it
all by yourself. God made sure you'd never need to change
alone. Accept His offer to adopt you into His family and
then spend each day growing with God.

. . . .

*I don't want to try to do the right thing without
help, Lord. Help me believe in You and then help
me grow up as one of Your brave children.*

CHARACTER OVER COMPROMISE

*Daniel made up his mind that he would
not make himself unclean.*
DANIEL 1:8

Daniel was taken captive to a kingdom called Babylon. They did things differently there—much differently than the way God said they should be done. Daniel could have done everything to blend in, but he chose something better.

Daniel chose character over compromise. For this young man, character meant following God even when it would've been easier not to. It meant doing something God wanted even when most people thought it was silly. It meant Daniel's choice would be in the spotlight. People would notice and they'd talk.

It was a big thing for Daniel to choose (to make up his mind) to not make sin his first choice. And Daniel could do that because God helped him with every choice he made. He was convinced God could help him—and then he watched God do impossible things for him. You can too.

Help me see that standing out is a good thing, God. May my character look like Yours. If You help me, it can.

HABIT AND CHARACTER

He who is right in his walk is sure in his steps.
PROVERBS 10:9

You know the way to your bedroom, right? You don't think much about how to get there. If you did pay attention, it might be twelve steps up the stairs, five more steps down the hall, then you turn right, and—*ta da*—you're in your room. But you don't usually count the steps or even think about what direction you're going; you just go to your room. Why? You know the way so well that you just know.

That's the idea behind good character. You accept help that only God can give. And you learn the way He wants you to go so well that following Him is just what you do. Character has a connection to habit and habit has a connection to faithfulness. Bad character means you're faithfully following bad habits. Good character means you're faithfully following good ones. This comes from learning all you can about God, then doing what you've learned.

I don't want to think that following You is something I do only when I feel like it, Father. I want to move in Your direction. You change my story—and You make it good.

WILLING TO WALK

When we have learned not to give up,
it shows we have stood the test. When we
have stood the test, it gives us hope.
ROMANS 5:4

You were reminded yesterday that you know your way to your room, but what if someone blindfolded you, spun you around, and asked you to find your room without any way to see? Would that make the task harder?

What if you were brought into a new house and told that you had a room waiting for you—all you needed to do was find it? Would it help to have someone show you?

God asks you to trust Him with everything you don't know. He will lead you. Ask Him.

Don't give up. Stand strong, even when you aren't sure which direction to go. Hold on to hope. God is willing to lead you. Be willing to walk with Him.

Some days are very hard, Lord. I get confused, and I'm not sure what to do. It can make me afraid, and I get discouraged. Help me remember that You'll lead me where I need to be—but that means I will need to move with You.

THINKING GOOD THOUGHTS

If there is anything good and worth giving thanks for, think about these things.

PHILIPPIANS 4:8

You can watch movies and TV shows on demand. You can find music and audiobooks in the same way. They just wait for you until you want them.

God offers better things than the world does, but you might be tempted to look elsewhere. The things you spend your brainpower on may not be true, respected, right, and pure—things God wants you to think about.

It's possible that when you search for "on demand" options, you're just looking for something more entertaining and fun than what you believe God offers. But God didn't create you to find satisfaction in worldly things. That's what you did before you became a Christian. Instead, do what Paul commanded in Galatians 5:16: "Let the Holy Spirit lead you in each step. Then you will not please your sinful old selves."

. . . .

Father, help me to think good thoughts today— ones that will please and honor You.

UPGRADED THINKING

*Keep your heart pure for out of it are
the important things of life.*
PROVERBS 4:23

Computers are wonderful, aren't they? You can play games on them, get information you might not have known before, and connect with other people. But not everything you see on your computer is good. Some of the information is false. Some of it is impure. And your computer can even end up with viruses from people with bad intentions.

Like your computer, you get information every day that you either accept or refuse. Some information can be very helpful, but other information can corrupt your thoughts. Bad thinking makes your heart less pure. It can spoil progress. But God even has that covered. He can turn bad things into good things. He can clean up what has become dirty. He can turn old habits into new opportunities. And He can start today. God's information, as found in His Word, is the way to upgrade your thinking.

· ·

*Create in me a pure heart, God. Give me a desire
to read Your Word every day so I can make good
decisions about what I will think about.*

TELL AND SHOW. . .AND TELL

*Show them how to live by your life
and by right teaching.*
TITUS 2:7

The *you* God made doesn't just affect you. Your choices and the character you display by your choices impact other people. That could be a younger brother or sister, friend, neighbor, cousin, or stranger. Boys learn from other boys, and the best example a boy can learn from will always be God. Show other boys how to live a great life by letting God teach you.

You might not want to be an example. You might just want to be left alone, but how would that help others grow in their godly character? Tell someone what you know about Jesus, show that person what new life in Christ looks like, and then continue learning so you can share that with others.

. . . .

*It seems easy to keep You a secret, Father. I can tell
You that I love You and then act like You don't matter
when I'm around others. You make a difference
so I want to tell others You make a difference.*

WHAT'S IMPORTANT

Do your best to add holy living to your faith.
Then add to this a better understanding. As you
have a better understanding, be able to say
no when you need to. Do not give up. And as
you wait and do not give up, live God-like.
2 PETER 1:5–6

God doesn't say, "Show me how hard you can work." He does seem to believe that if you really love Him, it will change what's important to you. When it changes what's important to you, then it changes what you do.

Some of the action words or phrases in today's verses include "Do your best," "Add to this," "Say no when you need to," "Do not give up," and "Live God-like." Following God requires effort. But as we make the right choices, the Holy Spirit empowers us.

The Christian life is like a mission with some responsibility. God can help you say no when you need to say it, be courageous when necessary, and understand why your choices should look like His.

I can do what You ask when You give me a brave heart, Lord. Make me courageous enough to take action as I boldly walk with You.

19

COME RUNNING

David was their shepherd with a heart that was right, and led them with good hands and wisdom.
PSALM 78:72

Just over a week ago, you read about Daniel, who was a man of character. Today you'll read about another man who was described as "a man who [was] pleasing to [God] in every way" (see 1 Samuel 13:14).

David was an imperfect king. But one thing was always true about David. When he broke God's law, he admitted he was wrong and asked God to help him make better choices.

Being a boy of character doesn't mean you'll never sin. But it does mean you will run toward God when you mess up, rather than away from Him. Come running, admit you were wrong, and accept God's forgiveness. Every single time.

King David wasn't so different from you. He broke God's rules too. He always came back to God. When you sin, you can too.

. . . .

I need to remember that when I fail to follow You, God, You always invite me to join You again. I don't want to even hesitate. I just want to come back. Thanks for loving me.

WALKING RIGHT

Your Word is a lamp to my feet and a light to my path.
PSALM 119:105

When you follow where God leads, He makes sure you know where to go. His Word directs your path as you go. The character word for this is *integrity*. This word means doing the right thing when nobody is watching, being confident that God is directing our steps.

God made you to grow in Him and honor Him in what you do. You're one of a kind, but you have the same job as every other person who follows God. Learn what He says so you can do what He wants.

You can try to become *you* without God, but something will always be missing. Why? Because your sinful heart will steer you off the path God wants you to walk on. Make following God your first and best choice.

· ·

Help me become a young man of integrity, Father. I want to follow the path You have put in front of me by staying in Your Word.

LIVING THE LIE

*The Lord hates lying lips, but those
who speak the truth are His joy.*
PROVERBS 12:22

Have you ever lied when a parent asked if you were lying? How did that make you feel?

Proverbs 12 tells the truth about lies—God isn't a fan. God knows everything about everyone who's ever lived. You can't lie to Him, expecting He'll believe it. God knows the truth even when you don't want to admit it. Lies waste time between the moment you break His rules and the moment He forgives you. Maybe part of the reason God hates lies is that they keep you from staying close to Him. It means you aren't learning because you're too busy making excuses for something you could easily admit. You refuse forgiveness because you want God and everyone you know to believe something that just isn't true.

God made you to be honest. No matter how well you lie, it will never fool God.

*May I tell You the truth, Lord, even when it means
I have to admit I've broken Your rules. I want to
find joy in honesty, no matter what it costs me.*

GOD-LIKE LIVING

*Growing strong in body is all right but growing
in God-like living is more important.*
1 TIMOTHY 4:8

If you're going to become good at a sport, it means you'll have to practice, practice, and then practice some more. You'll learn the basics and then continue practicing the skills. You'll learn about your opponents and determine how to do your best to stop them. It's why you have a coach and a team. A basketball game can't be won by one person.

The best example you can learn from team sports is that you don't have to compete by yourself. You can rely on other team members. In fact, if you don't, your team will suffer.

In life, you have God as a coach to help you learn what you need to find success.

God-like living that will mean more to you than any sports team you'll ever be a part of. That doesn't mean you can't enjoy sports, but sports can never be more important than being on God's team.

. . . .

*Teach me, God, and help me understand.
Walk with me and stay with me when I
can't keep up. Lead me and help me
recognize that Your way is the best path.*

RIGHT IS RIGHT

My children, let no one lead you in the wrong way.
The man who does what is right, is right with God
in the same way as Christ is right with God.

1 JOHN 3:7

Maybe you've heard it said that there's no wrong time to do the right thing. That's excellent advice. God doesn't want you to listen to anyone who says that doing something wrong is okay, even if you think it's for a good reason. It isn't.

Right is right and wrong is wrong. Mixing right with wrong can only lead to wrong. If there is a possibility of making an incorrect choice, then there must be correct options available, right? God said His Word is truth (see John 17:17). This is why it's so important to learn what God says is true. It allows you to see what isn't true.

. . . .

Teach me what is right, Father, so I can do the right thing. When I don't, then help me admit I was wrong. I never want to run from You.

LOVE IS STRANGE

Everything you do should be done in love.
1 CORINTHIANS 16:14

Love seems strange. It asks you to do what doesn't make sense. It asks you to give what you want to keep, do what you'd rather not do, and be kind when you'd rather be rude. God says everything you do should be done because of this strange thing called love.

It might seem like love should be something you feel—and it can be—but it's also the choice you need to make when you don't feel like it. Every person needs love, but some might be scared to show love because they worry it could mean they'll have less time, money, or things. Love is patient with people who annoy you, kind when you don't want to be, and humble when you want to brag.

Love isn't normal, it's strange—and that's what's so wonderful about it. The *you* that God made is to be someone who loves other people.

· ·

You love me, Lord, and that seems strange, but wonderful. Show me how to love others.

HOPE IS TRUST

Our hope comes from God. May He fill you with
joy and peace because of your trust in Him.
ROMANS 15:13

When you have faith in God, He can rescue you. When you believe in Him, He'll show you truth. When you trust Him, you'll discover joy.

When the Bible uses the word *hope*, it usually means trusting God. He knows what He's doing. He can turn bad situations into something very good. God can be trusted.

Joy shouts to the world, "I don't have to worry because God's in control. He always has been. He'll be in control again today." No wonder there's peace when you joyfully believe that God will never let you down.

If hope comes from God, and to hope means you trust, then God's actually giving you everything you need to hope (trust) in Him. God also gives us the gifts of peace and joy as we hope in Him.

God's been busy sending everything you need to build good character. Trust that His gifts are good and then use them to grow in hope, peace, and joy.

· ·

Give me hope and help me trust You, God.
Share Your peace and make me feel at home.

WHAT DO YOU THINK ABOUT MOST?

"You will keep the man in perfect peace whose mind is kept on You, because he trusts in You."
ISAIAH 26:3

What do you think about most? Sports, video games, or spending time with friends? Comic books, toys, or swimming? Computers, schoolwork, or movies? You can think about all kinds of things. But if you had a list of things you think about most, would God make your list? Where would He rank?

You'll be at your best when you keep God at the top of your list. If you don't trust certain people, it can be hard to think good things about them. You might not spend any time thinking about those you don't trust, or you might think a lot about them simply because you wonder what they are up to. But you can be sure that peace shows up when you think about God—because that shows that you trust Him.

Help me focus my thinking on You, Father. Send Your peace and help me trust You more today than I did yesterday.

BE GENTLE AND KIND

[Christians] must not speak bad of anyone,
and they must not argue. They should
be gentle and kind to all people.

TITUS 3:2

You might start sentences with, "Did you hear what. . ." or "You'll never believe what. . ." and then tell others something about someone that makes that person look bad. Those kinds of conversations are easy because they make you seem like a better person than whoever you're talking about.

God doesn't want you to do that. He also doesn't want you to argue with people. Instead of just telling you what you shouldn't do, God offers a different idea. If you want to speak bad about someone, God says you should be kind instead. If you want to argue with someone, then God says you should be gentle.

Christians are supposed to be different, and the things they do should be different too. Showing gentleness and kindness is the *you* He wants you to be.

. . . .

Being kind and gentle is hard, Lord. It's easier
to talk about other people when they aren't
around and it's always easier to argue.
Help me to be gentle and kind.

LEARNING PATIENCE

*I wait for the Lord. My soul waits
and I hope in His Word.*
PSALM 130:5

You can't wait for school to end (or start). You can't wait for Christmas (or your birthday). You can't wait to play football (or a video game). You just can't wait!

But sometimes, you *have* to wait. There's no choice. It's hard, isn't it? It's not what you want to do. You might be willing to wait for or put off things you don't want to do, like taking out the garbage, making your bed, or doing homework. But what about waiting for the Lord?

When you're having a bad day or wish your chores were finished, remember that God is always with You. He will give you peace, and He will comfort you as you trust Him. In fact, just before Jesus ascended into heaven, He said He would send the "Comforter," which is another name for the Holy Spirit. How cool is that?

* *

Help me to trust the Comforter, Lord, as I wait for You when times get tough. Thank You for caring so much that You sent the Holy Spirit to help Christians when they need it.

STAY ON THE PATH

Let your eyes look straight in front of you, and keep looking at what is in front of you. Watch the path of your feet, and all your ways will be sure.
PROVERBS 4:25–26

You can't get to your bedroom from the kitchen by just wishing you were there. You need to move your feet. You can't win a football game from the sidelines. You need to learn how to play the game. You can't win a race without being in the race.

Christians can sometimes get distracted when we look at what the world has to offer. Today's verses tell us to keep looking forward, which means to stay on the path of truth and holiness. We do this through *perseverance*, which means doing hard things (with the Holy Spirit's help) that lead to a win for God's kingdom. If you wander off the path of truth and holiness, you aren't in the game God wants you to play.

Stay focused on what the Bible says, no matter what everyone else is saying or doing.

. . . .

Keep my feet pointed in Your direction, Father— and help me persevere to stay on the right path.

MEEKNESS SEEMS BETTER

*Those who have no pride will be given
the earth. And they will be happy.*
PSALM 37:11

The Bible says you should be *meek*. If that's a new word for you, then you should know the word means a couple of things. The first is not thinking that you're better or more important than other people. The second is to believe that God knows more than you so you should always believe and follow His directions, not your own.

To be meek means that you have God's strength but refuse to show off. It means you have His help but refuse to take credit for anything. And it means you have God's love but refuse to keep it to yourself.

When you choose to be meek, you're happier and life Is better. You'll probably like this more than feeling sad and disappointed. God wants meekness to describe who you are.

. . . .

*I don't want to think I'm better than others, Lord.
Help me to believe that You know more than I
do and will always help me when I ask.*

THE LEARNING THING

Wisdom is with those who have no pride.
PROVERBS 11:2

You were not created to make choices without good information. God wants you to know as much about Him as possible. That happens when you read the Bible. A couple of wonderful things happen when you make the choice to learn from God. The first is that you get to discover what's important to Him. The second is that you get to understand how those things can change the way you do things.

No one gets to decide that they're smarter than God. No one gets to say that what God says is no longer true. No one is as important as God. Wisdom knows this is true. Understanding says it's a bad choice to challenge God. And being humble means you give credit to God for the things you're learning.

You can do more than just think that God is good. You can learn just how good God actually is. You can read examples of His goodness, explore why His goodness is important, and then choose to use this wisdom every day.

Wisdom comes from You, God. I want Your wisdom. I want to understand You so I can be like You.

THE FRUIT TREE

*The fruit that comes from having the Holy Spirit
in our lives is: love, joy, peace, not giving up,
being kind, being good, having faith, being gentle,
and being the boss over our own desires.*
GALATIANS 5:22–23

Can you imagine a fruit tree that has apples, pears, plums, and oranges? It may sound like a crazy science experiment, but the truth is you have a spiritual tree growing in your life—and it contains all kinds of spiritual fruit. Today's verses give you a list of the fruit that Christians have inside them. It is growing in you because of the Holy Spirit. This fruit is a gift so you can be the real you—the *you* God created you to be.

Of course, having the fruit of the Spirit growing inside you doesn't mean you won't mess up sometimes. But it does mean you will ask God to forgive you and then trust Him to continue to work in your life.

. . . .

Forgive me, Father, for the times when I don't show the fruit of the Spirit in my behavior. Please continue to shape me into the boy You created me to be.

COMPASSION ISLAND

*The people on the island were very
kind to us. It was raining and cold.
They made a fire so we could get warm.*

ACTS 28:2

Luke was a doctor whom God used to write the books of Luke and Acts. He was on a ship with Paul when a horrible storm broke out and left them stranded on the island of Malta. Some people were hearing about Jesus for the first time when Paul spoke, which was incredible—but these people already knew a lot about compassion. They showed great concern for the hard things Paul and Luke were going through by starting a fire for them so they could get warm.

What can you do today to show compassion for other people? If you aren't sure where to begin, watch and listen for their needs, then follow through and help them. It can make all the difference.

. . . .

*When I see people who need help, Lord, it's easy
to think someone else will do it. Help me to be
as compassionate as the people from Malta.*

DON'T FORGET THE THANKS

Let us give thanks all the time to God through Jesus Christ. Our gift to Him is to give thanks. Our lips should always give thanks to His name.
HEBREWS 13:15

Today's verse might make you think differently about giving thanks than you ever have. The writer says that our gift to God is to give thanks. And the writer says we should give thanks *always*.

You were created to be thankful. Even when bad days come? Thank God that it wasn't worse. Even when you didn't get your way? Thank Him for the wisdom to know what you really need. Even when people are mean to you? Thank Him that He loves you more than the person who is being mean to you.

Being thankful helps other people see you're different and that God is doing something great inside you.

Stop me from complaining, God. I want to be thankful in all things. And I want to give You the gift today of thanking You for everything You do.

35

DON'T GET MAD

Try to understand other people. Forgive each other.
If you have something against someone, forgive him.
COLOSSIANS 3:13

People will do things you'll never understand. It could be things they say or do, or words they say to others that are unkind and untrue—even about you. The Bible says we should not get mad when this happens. And we should not get even. God says we should forgive because He does that for you.

Sometimes people hurt inside. They're angry about things that aren't your fault, but their anger can reach out and hurt you when you get too close. They might not even mean to be rude or mean, but that's how it felt. Right? When Jesus was dying on the cross and people were saying mean things about Him, He said, "Father, forgive them. They do not know what they are doing" (Luke 23:34).

If you don't forgive people who wrong you, then you can hang onto the hurt. And it becomes easier to hurt other people. Be the *you* God created you to be—forgive.

. . . .

***People who do mean things don't always know
what they're doing, Father. Remind me to
forgive them when they do something wrong.***

HAPPY FOR WHAT YOU HAVE

*A God-like life gives us much when we
are happy for what we have.*
1 TIMOTHY 6:6

Make a list of what you have. It might include clothes, toys, video games, tablets, a bed, a dresser, a television—and don't forget your Bible. You didn't bring any of those things with you when you were born. Someone gave you those things. Someone works to make sure you have food, water, and a roof to sleep under. You may not have everything you want, but you have all the things you need. God says that when you follow Him, you can be happy for the things you actually have instead of angry because you don't have what you want.

There's a big difference. Sometimes you can feel like you don't have anything because you know someone who has more than you have. You have air, so breathe deeply. You have something to drink, so be refreshed. You get tired, so sleep well. Be happy for what you have.

. . . .

I hate to feel like I'm missing out, Lord. I want to think of what I have, rather than what I don't. And thank You for sharing it with me.

WORK TOGETHER

Work for the things that make peace and help each other become stronger Christians.
ROMANS 14:19

Some people can come into a room and make every other person so uncomfortable that the whole group wants to fight. Maybe you know someone like that. Adults might say it's someone who "stirs the pot." God says you should not be like that guy.

Find ways to bring peace to those around you. Encourage other people to follow Christ. Don't try to make people angry or unhappy. Some people do this because they think it's fun to make people mad. God says that never helps bring peace and it never teaches anyone a good way to grow as a Christian. When you choose to make things hard for other people, it just wastes time that could be spent helping someone, following God, and finding peace. Work together. Walk together. Become wise together.

You don't want me to try to do everything on my own, God. You help me and You bring others to help. Let me learn the value of the help You give.

GOD MADE YOU *YOU*

God made man in His own likeness.
GENESIS 1:27

God made you *you*. You're not an accident. You aren't leftover parts. God made you on purpose, just the way you are. He loved the thought of you, so He took those thoughts and made *you*.

People don't build a house without a plan. A car cannot be assembled if no one designed it. Did you know you were on God's heart before you cried for the first time?

You're not like anyone else, and nobody is like you. God has more than enough ideas when it comes to the way He designs each person. He can create you and everyone else in your house differently, and He *still* has more ideas about how He'll create others.

If it seems like we keep saying God made you, then you're getting the point. It's a celebration-worthy thing to say. It's important to believe, and it will change the way you think about yourself and the God who loves you.

. . . .

Thank You for making me ME, Father. I don't need to try to be anyone else. Help m understand what You planned for me. Then help me to do it.

A FUTURE DIFFERENCE STARTS TODAY

"I know the plans I have for you," says the Lord, "plans for well-being and not for trouble, to give you a future and a hope."

JEREMIAH 29:11

If you put a toy boat on a lake, it won't be long before that boat is far away from the shore or sitting at the bottom of the lake. You wouldn't plan to lose the toy, but if you didn't pay attention, it would get away from you.

God doesn't have that problem. You're never too far away from Him to be found. He knows where He'd like you to go, and He's always been the best at rescuing boys like you.

He wants you to believe His ideas are the best. If you obey Him, His ideas will make you a better person and you won't find yourself in trouble. The future is better because of God's ideas. Trust that this is true.

I want to believe You have a better plan, Lord. I can have good plans or even great plans, but Yours will always be better. Your way is good, and Your plan is best.

TRUST HIS PURPOSE

Christ made everything in the heavens and on the earth. He made everything that is seen and things that are not seen. . . . All things are held together by Him.
COLOSSIANS 1:16–17

The world is full of unusual creatures, like the star-nosed mole, red-lipped batfish, yeti crabs, blobfish, and the narwhal. But no matter how strange they may seem to you, they are beautiful to God. He made them—on purpose.

There are unusual plants, rocks, and planets too. God made those on purpose. He made everything. God even made the things you can only see under a microscope. He made things you can't see at all. He's never forgotten or abandoned any of the things He's made. Every day He tells the sun to rise, the moon to set, and the skies to invite you to the day.

Because God does that, you should never doubt that you've been made with a purpose. You may not fully understand your purpose right now—but keep trusting God and you'll learn.

I need to remember that the things that are different about me are Your gift, God. Thank You for making me 100 percent me.

PLANET PURPOSE

The heavens are telling of the greatness of God and the great open spaces above show the work of His hands.

PSALM 19:1

Did you know that the earth is the only planet in our solar system that can produce fire? Fire needs oxygen, and the earth has lots of that. The other planets don't. Each planet has its own unique qualities. Some spin faster than others. Gravity is different on each planet. The color of the sky on these planets can be a color that isn't blue. And each one of those planets, each star and asteroid seems to shout to you from the sky, "Hey, look, God made me. Pay attention to Him."

God took care of every detail in this world that He made you to live on. He paid attention to the space around you, and He invites you to look up in wonder at the pinpoint of stars and the glowing orbs of planets. It pleased Him that this would please you.

. . . .

I look up and I see Your good work, Father. You did this for me, and I believe You've done even more. I want others to discover Your good work in me.

A PART OF YOUR STORY

*Even before the world was made, God chose
us for Himself because of His love.*
EPHESIANS 1:4

Before the world started spinning, before the mountains stretched skyward, and before the ocean waves began to roll, God knew you and looked forward to meeting you.

God loved you before oxygen, water, and food. He loved you more than any planet, animal, or bird. He loved you more than you can love anything. God loves you. He doesn't just put up with you. He never replies, "Not *you* again." He wants the best for you. He wants to be part of your story. He's been waiting to help you. Will you let Him?

God doesn't demand that you let Him help, but He's willing to guide you. He wants you to choose Him. He doesn't want you to feel alone. You've felt that way before, right? You've wondered if anyone really cared about you. You've wondered where you fit in. This is God's answer: "Before the world was made. I chose you because I love you!"

* * *

It's good to be wanted, Lord. It's awesome to be loved. It's incredible that You do both—for me.

SEEKING PEOPLE

*God knew from the beginning who would
put their trust in Him. So He chose them
and made them to be like His Son.*
ROMANS 8:29

God isn't pushy, but He never stops trying to reach you. Do you want a good idea of what to do with your life? Well, God has answers. You should become friends with God.

Everyone needs to know Him. That's exactly what God wants, but He also knows that some people won't choose Him as a forever friend. That has never stopped God from seeking people who need better direction. We all do.

God never hides from people who look for Him. He never refuses answers when someone wants to know Him. If you seek Him, He can be found.

You have a purpose. The moment you trust in God, you will begin to learn why God created you the way He did. The best journey you'll ever take starts with this step.

. . . .

*I'm the one who needs You, God. I want to know
You, walk with You, and grow in You today
and every day for the rest of my life.*

BEYOND BAD THINGS

We know that God makes all things work together for the good of those who love Him and are chosen to be a part of His plan.
ROMANS 8:28

Bad things happen. That's not news, is it? Bad things have probably happened to you or someone you love. You want it to be different, but people get to make their own choices. Sometimes the choices they make are bad.

When something bad happens to you, that doesn't have to be the end of your story. God can take every one of those bad things and turn them into something good. It's like a flower seed that lands in the crack of a sidewalk. It doesn't seem like a perfect location, but somehow, the flower grows. When bad things happen, it is best to allow God to take over.

The *you* God made needs to know for sure that He can be trusted with all the bad things you'll ever face.

I hate bad things, Father, but I love You. Help me trust that good can come from bad things when You're in charge.

BE THAT NEW PERSON

Do not act like the sinful people of the world. Let God change your life. First of all, let Him give you a new mind. Then you will know what God wants you to do.

ROMANS 12:2

Some people wear camouflage to blend in when they're outdoors. They don't want to be noticed. You might wear camouflage too. It may not be the clothing you wear, but maybe you hide the good things God is doing in you. You might not want people to think you're foolish for following God. But when you do what other people do, especially when those people don't love God, then you're telling other people that you agree with them. They might believe you think God isn't worth trusting.

God made you to stand out, stand up, and stand strong. God started making you a new person from the moment you accepted His rescue. That new person is thankful for the new life. That new person wants other people to know about God. That new person thinks new thoughts. Be that new person.

. . . .

Give me the courage I need, Lord. Give me Your wisdom. Give me the strength to be a new person.

FINISHING THE JOB

The Lord will finish the work He started for me.
O Lord, Your loving-kindness lasts forever.
PSALM 138:8

New life in Christ begins with new information. This information, which comes from the Bible, challenges poor thinking. And once God starts making you a new person, He has no intention of abandoning the work He started. In fact, He won't. Some people indeed decide they won't cooperate with God, but that doesn't mean He stops working. His kindness does something special inside you and that kindness brings you closer to Him, even when you might want to stay away.

King David wrote Psalm 138. David knew from experience that God never abandoned Him. So he watched God's kindness and couldn't help thanking God for taking bad things and making them good. He's doing the same thing for you.

. . . .

When I became a Christian, Lord, You made me a
new person in Christ. Please don't stop. I want
new life, new thinking, and new gratitude.
Don't abandon me. Help me stay close to You.

HONOR AND OBEDIENCE

The last word, after all has been heard,
is: Honor God and obey His Laws.
This is all that every person must do.
ECCLESIASTES 12:13

Ecclesiastes 12:13 says that learning what God wants is an important lesson. If you really want to know what you were created to do, then this is the verse you can always come back to. Before, during, and after you learn about the character traits God wants you to have, you should know that God made you to honor Him and do what He asks you to do.

When you want to be more like God by doing what He says you should do, it means something very special has happened in your life. It means you believe Him, trust Him, and follow Him. Maybe that's why this verse is so important. When you do these two things, it means life makes more sense—even when things are hard.

You are more important than anything, Father.
I want to honor You. And I want to obey
You because I know it pleases You.

48

STRENGTH WHERE IT MATTERS

*I can do all things because Christ
gives me the strength.*
PHILIPPIANS 4:13

Following God doesn't give you permission to do what you want. But He does give us the strength, courage, and ability to do what *He* wants. As you honor and obey God, even when life is tough, then you'll begin to see what Philippians 4:13 is talking about.

God has created you for a purpose. Talk to older Christians about what that purpose might be. They will offer you guidance. When they do, begin to explore what they suggest. They might see that you have a heart for helping or encouraging other people. And they will make suggestions for ways you can do that. As you do, God will give you the strength to make a difference.

- -

*I want to be strong enough to do what You want
me to do, Lord. Strengthen me, Lord. I want to go
where You want me to go. Help me to follow.*

ANSWER THE QUESTION

Whatever you do, do everything to honor God.
1 CORINTHIANS 10:31

You'll make choices today. You made one when you picked up this book. You'll make another when you're finished. Hopefully there will be enough information that you'll make more good choices.

Some choices you make will move you closer to God. Other choices will pull you further away. You can test every decision in one very simple way. Ask yourself if what you are planning to do honors God or breaks one of His commands. *That's it.* That's a tool God has given you to make great decisions. It won't have anything to do with how a choice makes you feel, and it has nothing to do with the opinions of others.

Does your choice honor God? That's the question you need to answer. It's a question God can help you answer.

· ·

I've made wrong choices, God. I know this because some choices have not honored You. I want to honor You going forward.

NO WAITING

While we were still sinners, Christ died for us.
ROMANS 5:8

Knowing you break God's rules should make you thankful that God made a way for boys to come to Jesus and become guilt-free. This is important because if you think you don't sin—that you don't break God's rules—then you're kidding yourself (see 1 John 1:8).

The only way God could view you as someone who has no guilt was to pay the price for sin. That price was death. God's Son, Jesus, did that for you. Jesus didn't wait until you were super smart so you could figure out how to stop sinning. He didn't wait for you to do anything. He just took care of it.

This rescue from the penalty of every sin was all about what only He could do. It has nothing to do with how good you've been—or will be. This is how much you matter to God. He loved you so much that He sent His only Son to die for you.

. . . .

You made a way for me to be rescued, Father. Thank You.

BECAUSE GOD MADE YOU

*The prayer from the heart of a man
right with God has much power.*
JAMES 5:16

God says you have worth simply because He made you. When you know who He is and what He has done for you, then He would love to hear from you. This happens when you pray.

As a follower of God, there's more importance to your prayer. You know who you are praying to. You know God because you're friends with Him and what He says means something important to you. Your prayers are powerful because they prove you're learning from the God who says your friendship is worth it.

The *you* God made you to be is someone who talks with Him. You share all the hurt, happiness, and hope you have inside. You learn what God wants by reading the Bible. You do what He asks you to do. These are good ways to show God how important His friendship is to you.

I want to keep speaking with you, Lord. I want to keep reading what You say. I want to be friends. Keep me on the narrow path that leads to You.

FREE IN CHRIST

Christ made us free. Stay that way.
GALATIANS 5:1

You've probably read about slavery. In case you aren't familiar with it, slavery means a person is forced to do things he or she doesn't want or shouldn't have to do. On the other hand, when you're free, you get to do something better. The Bible calls every person a "slave to sin." After you become a Christian, you don't have to sin. You will desire to sin, but you don't need to give in to it. Never believe that you do.

The freedom you can experience as a Christian is the freedom to do good, to obey God, and to enjoy a friendship with God. This all happens because you're considered worthy—and free.

People who have made other people slaves don't really care for their slaves, but God cares enough about you to know your name. He pays attention to the things you do and invites you to be part of His family.

. . . .

A slave owner might treat me like property they own, God. But the freedom You offer treats me like we're the best of friends. I love that about You.

LOOKING OUT FOR YOU

*[God saved] us from the punishment of sin.
It was not because we worked to be right
with God. It was because of His loving-
kindness that He washed our sins away.*

TITUS 3:5

Parents might see their children nearing a dangerous situation and take action before anything bad happens. Most boys aren't even aware of how often this takes place. Like a good parent, God knows when you're headed toward a bad choice, and He fixes things before you break even one rule.

You might think you need to pay Him back and do a certain number of good things to make up for doing something bad, but He wants you to know you can never make things right on your own. You can be forgiven though because God loves you.

*I don't need to try harder to make You value me,
Father. You already do. I should do good things but
not because it makes You think better of me. I want
to be right with You because You made that possible.*

EVERY SINGLE PERSON

[Jesus] said to them, "You are to go to all the world and preach the Good News to every person."
MARK 16:15

God doesn't come to you privately, tell you that you're loved, and then say, "Keep this between you and Me. I don't love just anyone." Once you accept His offer of rescue, He says something like "Now, go and tell everyone else. They need this good news too."

It should make you feel good that God cared so much about you that He made sure you could be rescued. And that should make you want to tell others that they, too, can be rescued—even people you don't like. You get to be someone who connects other people to God's rescue plan. Isn't that exciting?

God doesn't pick and choose who He'll love. He didn't just pay the price of sin for *some* humans. He loves every single person who's ever lived. And He would love to see every single person who's ever lived love Him too.

. . . .

I want to remember that You love everyone, Lord. Because You value everyone, help me value them too.

55

SETTLED

What starts wars and fights among you?
Is it not because you want many things
and are fighting to have them?

JAMES 4:1

People can make you mad—really mad. Maybe they meant to or maybe it was an accident but after they said what they said, well, you're angry. They realize you're angry and might think you're wrong, so they get angry.

Once everyone is upset with each other, no one sees the other person as valuable. You want to be right. They want to be right. No one seems interested in anything other than a fight. The more you think about what the other person did or said, the angrier you get and the less interested you are in learning what God thinks.

Ask yourself these questions the next time someone makes you mad: Would God treat that person the way you treat them? Does God treat you the way others treat you? Let the answer to these questions change your choice, calm your anger, and inspire forgiveness.

I want to think differently about arguments,
God. Help me be patient and to
remember You value everyone.

COMPARISONS

*I ask each one of you not to think more of himself
than he should think. Instead, think in the right way
toward yourself by the faith God has given you.*
ROMANS 12:3

It can be very easy to look at how you're doing as a Christian and then look at other guys you know and think, "Wow, I am pretty amazing at this whole Christianity thing." You might even take the next step and point out the things you seem to do better than most Christian guys you know. It doesn't usually end there. You move on to thinking that these other people should look to you as their example and do better.

God says *Jesus* is your example. Everyone can do better. Everyone needs to be forgiven. Everyone is worth the same amount to God. His love is for everyone. His rescue plan is for everyone. No one is left out or overlooked. No one is considered better or worse because everyone needs the same forgiveness and love.

. . . .

**There's no use in comparing myself to
others, Father. I'm not better than anyone.
Everyone needs You, including me.**

YOUR RESPONSE

If you show loving-kindness, God will show loving-kindness to you when you are told you are guilty.
JAMES 2:13

God made the rules. He asks you to follow them. He also said in Romans 3:23 that you would break His rules. When you break even one rule, you're as guilty as if you broke them all. This could sound like very bad news but read James 2:13 again.

You are worth so much to Him. He wants you to know that when you're kind the way He's kind, then forgiveness and mercy are gifts He wants to give when you break His rules. These gifts may not be possible if you want to see others punished, even if you still want God to show kindness to you. Give the same gifts God gives you. If someone needs help knowing a better way to do things, then let God do the teaching instead of doing your best to get that person in trouble.

. . . .

Your kindness is a good reason to celebrate, Lord. This same kindness is a good thing to share. Help me celebrate. Help me share.

TO ALL

Do not look on one person as more important than another.
JAMES 2:1

God never asks you to do anything He doesn't already do Himself. Example? When God said you shouldn't look on one person as more important than another, this is exactly what He already does. God doesn't play favorites. His love is for all. His rescue is available to all. His forgiveness is by request for all. Not only to a few, some, or many—*all.*

Some people think they can ignore people who don't seem interested in God. Tomorrow you'll read about one man who was rescued when no one could even imagine Him following Jesus. Maybe you know somebody like that. But don't give up on that person. Make sure everybody you know hears how Jesus can save them. Don't play favorites, and don't leave people out.

. . . .

You're in the business of good news, God. You want everyone to find You. I don't want to stand in their way by thinking one person is more important than another.

A NOON MEETING

[Paul said,] "I was near Damascus.
All at once, about noon, I saw a bright light
from heaven shining around me."

ACTS 22:6

It was lunchtime in Damascus. Maybe Paul was hungry or tired. Mostly, he was surprised. This surprise changed everything for Paul. Before this, he had hurt Christians. Paul was good at his job. Nobody thought he'd ever be anything but mean to Christians. But that was before a noon meeting with Jesus.

The first question Jesus asked Paul was, "Why do you work so hard against Me?" (Acts 22:7) Paul didn't have a good answer. He might have thought, "Why *am* I so mean?" But Jesus wasn't mean to Paul. Instead of fighting with Jesus, Paul decided to accept His rescue plan. That's when Paul's life changed. What caused the change in Paul? Maybe it was kindness. Maybe it was knowing that Jesus thought he had value. Either way, Paul realized he needed help.

Knowing You think I have value can change
my future, Father. I don't have to impress
You with good behavior, compare myself to
others, or fight against Your goodness.

HEART INSPECTION

*Look through me, O God, and know my heart. Try me
and know my thoughts. See if there is any sinful way
in me and lead me in the way that lasts forever.*

PSALM 139:23–24

Do you trust God enough to allow Him to find all the sinful things you've ever done? The things other people know about and the things no other person knows but you? You may have tried hiding your sin for a very long time and it's not helping you. Even if you haven't admitted what you've done, God already knows. He's been waiting to forgive you. He's been waiting for you to confess it. He's been waiting for you to come close again.

Guilt doesn't have to hang out at your house, but as long as you hide the truth that you've broken God's rules, you'll feel guilty. Give God permission to inspect your heart and remind you of the broken rules. Admit what you did, and God will forgive.

. . . .

*You say I'm worth forgiving, Lord. You don't want
me to hide my bad choices from You. You want
me to be honest with You. Help me to always
be honest in my relationship with You.*

GOD'S PERSONAL UPDATES

Trust in the Lord with all your heart, and do not trust in your own understanding.
PROVERBS 3:5

God has a plan—trust it. You have a plan—*question it.* God understands everything perfectly. There's a lot you'll never completely understand. God knows how things will end up. The best you can do is guess.

Many people pray and they're pretty sure their idea is a good one, but they rarely want to know God's plan. They often tell God what they want to do and hope He agrees with them.

Proverbs 3:5 makes sure you know God can be trusted while your thinking (without His help) cannot. God wants to meet with you. And He wants to tell you what He thinks. Read the Bible to get His personal updates, and He will speak to you.

* * *

You know many things that I don't, God. Teach me to follow Your directions so my understanding will be in line with Yours.

GOD IS ALWAYS RIGHT

*Agree with Him in all your ways,
and He will make your paths straight.*
PROVERBS 3:6

God is always right—even when you don't agree with Him. That has always been true. Some people think that as time has passed, God has relaxed His rules. But God doesn't make mistakes.

People break God's rules every day. And every second someone needs to be forgiven.

What if you agreed that God is always right? How would it change things for you? Proverbs 3:6 suggests that it makes His plan for you easier to follow.

God will always welcome your questions, but He is also pleased with your obedience. You can go further as a Christian much faster when you trust where God is leading you. After all, He knows what He's doing.

. . . .

I want to agree that Your way is good, Father. Sometimes that's hard for me because I can't see my future as clearly as You can. Give me the courage to walk with You, believing that Your way is perfect.

SHOW ME, LORD

*I will show you and teach you in the way
you should go. I will tell you what to do.*
PSALM 32:8

When you think God is hiding and doesn't really care about you, read Psalm 32:8. Be encouraged. God doesn't tell you to figure things out on your own. He wants to show you, teach you, and tell you which steps you should take.

You're not alone. You never have been. You are who you are because God is who He is. You need help, and He helps. You need hope, and He offers more than you ask for. You need forgiveness, and He's ready to forgive you.

God wants to show you, teach you, and tell you everything you need to know. He wants you to live a life that is bigger and more important than you could ever imagine on your own.

Your plan for me doesn't have to be a secret, Lord. You want me to know even more than I want to know. Show me. Teach me. Tell me. Help me to pay attention and then walk in Your ways.

RECOGNIZE THE VOICE

*"My sheep hear My voice and
I know them. They follow Me."*
JOHN 10:27

You know some voices the moment you hear them. Some are unfamiliar. Some make you afraid. Some feel like a welcome home. When God speaks, He says some will recognize His voice and follow Him.

This is important because it should remind you that God wants to help you. He wants to be so close to you that you'll know when He's offering help, encouragement, and wisdom. He wants you to invite Him to help.

God's plans not only include you but invite you to participate. You are the only one who can do what God wants you to do. You can't ask someone else to do your job. When you recognize God's voice, it's a reminder that He knows you. It's a reminder that He has a plan for you. It's a reminder that you should go where He leads.

. . . .

Every day I'm learning that You care more for me than I thought, God. You want me close. Help me recognize when You're teaching me.

CLEAN INSIDE

*[Jesus] gave Himself so His people could
be clean and want to do good.*
TITUS 2:14

God's plan is so different from the way most people do things. Humans like to brag about the good they do for others. People might talk about how much money they have given to the poor or how they helped someone with a task. But people are not good naturally.

God says the only real way for people to want to do good is if they could be forgiven for all the sins they have committed. Only He could think of such a good idea. When you've done bad things, it's easy to think that if you just did more good things, then everything would be all right. When will you do enough good? Who decides when you've done enough? How does this help you see a need for God?

Do you see the problem with trying to clean yourself up with good works?

I can't clean myself up, Father. No person can do it for me, and I can't ignore the need to be clean. But when You make me clean, You can help me do the right thing.

DONE RIGHT

*The Holy Spirit speaks to us and tells our
spirit that we are children of God.*
ROMANS 8:16

It's easy to think that if anything is going to get done, then you have to do it. Hard work is important. As a Christian, you should work hard because you represent Jesus to people who don't believe in Him. But you can never work hard or do enough good things to earn your salvation.

God gave you the right to become a family member and then gave you the power (everything you need) to become His son. How amazing is that? You experience this power when you trust (believe) in Christ who paid for all your sins with His death on the cross. If you could earn your salvation, then you wouldn't need the Holy Spirit. But you can't, and you *need* the Holy Spirit!

God is the only one who can truthfully say that if something is going to be done right, then He needs to do it Himself.

. . . .

***Thanks for making it possible to follow You,
Lord, when I didn't deserve that at all.***

A REALLY GOOD PLAN

If a man belongs to Christ, he is a new person.
The old life is gone. New life has begun.
2 CORINTHIANS 5:17

The *you* God made you to be is not the same person who came home from the hospital as a baby. God designed you to want to be a new person. He wants you to leave all the bad things you've done behind. He paid for those sins with His Son's life. Now He wants you to live differently.

Most people don't change overnight, so don't be surprised if it seems easier to do things the old way. But when you do, ask God for help. He will, you know.

The more time you spend doing things the way God wants them done, the more you'll want to keep doing things that way. New life tells the old way of doing things that it's time to leave. That's God's plan—and it's a good one.

· ·

It seems easier to do things I'm familiar with, God. You want me to do things a new way though. Help me learn Your new way.

NO WAITING REQUIRED

Let all kings fall down at His feet,
and all nations serve Him.
PSALM 72:11

God's plan is that everyone (including you) would choose Him and that people would learn from Him and do what He does. But even if people do not follow Him, God made another plan that's also a promise. At some point, every single person who's ever lived will finally understand that God is exactly who He said He is. All people will honor God someday—even if they never chose to follow Him. But sadly, if they wait until judgment day to do so, it will be too late for them to go to heaven.

As a Christian, you can honor God today. The new life God gives you also offers you the chance to get closer to Him every day. Do more than just think about God though. Honor Him with your actions. And follow Him with everything you have.

. . . .

I want to honor You today with my actions,
Father. I worship and adore You.
Wherever You lead me today, I will follow.

SPEAK

*Sing to the Lord, all the earth. Tell the good
news of His saving power from day to day.
Tell of His greatness among the nations.
Tell of His great works among all the people.*
1 CHRONICLES 16:23–24

If you've ever had a role in a school play or musical performance in which you had to get up by yourself in front of everybody, then you know how scary that can be. Maybe you didn't feel like you even had a good enough voice to be up in front of everybody. The Christian life can feel like that sometimes too.

Today's passage encourages you to sing to the whole earth in a different way. In other words, it wants you to have the good news on the tip of your tongue, ready to speak it to anybody who will listen. The Holy Spirit will help you. You don't have to be afraid to explain how your friends and relatives can be saved through the death of Jesus on the cross.

. . . .

*I don't want to be afraid to talk about You,
Lord. I want to share the good news with others.
People need to know You're wonderful.*

70

TELL THEM

How can they put their trust in Him if they have not heard of Him? And how can they hear of Him unless someone tells them?

ROMANS 10:14

Today's verse asks a very good question: "How can they (all people) put their trust in Him (God) if they haven't heard of Him?" This question seems to say that people need someone to say something for God so they can have the opportunity to trust Him. This verse continues by asking, "How can they (other people) hear of Him (God) unless someone tells them?" This is where you come in.

Somebody told you about Jesus. Now it's your turn to tell others. God could use your words to encourage more people to trust Him with their souls. You get to be a part of that—just by saying something good about God.

. . . .

Staying quiet about You is easy, God. I'm afraid some people might ask questions and I won't know the answers. Help me to trust You to tell me exactly what I need to say as I talk to others about You.

A VERY SPECIFIC JOB

*Jesus said to them again, "May you have peace.
As the Father has sent Me, I also am sending you."*
JOHN 20:21

When you grow up and get a job, your boss will give you work to do each day. He or she will give you the training you need to do a good job, then expect you to do it. You probably won't do everything perfectly right away, but you will learn over time.

Jesus taught people who followed Him. He gave them a job. He sent them to do that job. He still sends people to do a very specific job—to tell people about Him. You won't do it perfectly right away, but that's okay. The Holy Spirit is inside you and He will teach you how to go out and tell others about Jesus.

. . . .

Lord Jesus, I want the peace You speak about in today's verse as I tell others about You. Send me out in confidence that You are always with me.

WHAT HE WANTS YOU TO DO

*The mind of a man plans his way,
but the Lord shows him what to do.*
PROVERBS 16:9

What do you want to be when you grow up? You've been asked that before, right? Maybe you have an idea and maybe you don't have a clue. Some might say, "You have plenty of time to figure it out so maybe it's not worth worrying about."

They're right, you know. You don't need to worry about your future because God knows what He wants you to do, and He can help you learn how to do it. You can make all the plans you want as long as you're willing to let God make changes to your plan.

Since God made you, He knows you better than anyone—even better than you know yourself. If you let Him help, then His plans can become your plans. His way can become your way. His gifts can become useful to you every day.

When it's time, help me understand what You want me to do for You, Lord. Teach me every day and help me trust that Your plans will always make my life better.

73

HE'S NEVER AFRAID

"The Lord is the One Who goes before you. He will be with you. He will be faithful to you and will not leave you alone. Do not be afraid or troubled."

DEUTERONOMY 31:8

You can't go somewhere God hasn't already been. He walks beside you as a friend. He walks before you as a guide. He walks behind you as a protector.

You never need to be afraid to walk with God. He forgives, He accepts, and He's faithful to you. God never pretends He doesn't know you, He won't leave you behind, and He won't ever make you do what He asks without helping you.

God's plan is that you follow Him successfully. He wants to see you do what He asks, but He knows you can't do it alone. He will bring people to help you, and He'll help you. You can leave fear behind because God walks with you—and He's never afraid.

* * *

I can trust You, God. I don't want to doubt that You'll help me, but if I do, would You please remind me that when I walk with You, You're walking with me?

74

SAFER TO TRUST GOD

He who trusts in his own heart is a fool,
but he who walks in wisdom will be kept safe.
PROVERBS 28:26

How important are the things you think about? That is a very good question. In fact, it's a question you should look at over the next few days. Start today.

If thinking about God is something you only do in church on the weekend, then your thoughts are on the cares of this world. You are trying to live without any godly instructions. God says it's foolish to trust what you think, but it's safe to trust in the wisdom that comes from Him.

If you want to spend more time thinking about God, then read the Bible often. And spend time with people who follow God. They can show you how they learned to concentrate on God.

. . . .

Help me pay attention to You, Father. I don't
mean to ignore You, but sometimes I do.
Keep me safe by keeping my mind on You.

NEW SOCKS

Put away the old person you used to be. Have nothing to do with your old sinful life. It was sinful because of being fooled into following bad desires.
EPHESIANS 4:22

✩

People don't usually choose something to wear to an important event by looking in the dirty laundry pile. Socks you've worn more than once shouldn't be your go-to pair next week. When you have a new shirt, why would you dig out the dirty one you played football in last weekend?

When a boy like you finds God, it can and should change you. God wants you to stop living the way you used to. In fact, God wants you to have nothing to do with your old choices. He doesn't want you to be the same person you used to be. He's given you a new identity. He's written your name in His book of family members. His plan for you includes new choices.

. . . .

The choices I used to make weren't great, Lord. Help me to make better ones now.

HELPFUL? OR CARELESS?

"It is not what goes into a man's mouth that makes his mind and heart sinful. It is what comes out of a man's mouth that makes him sinful."
MATTHEW 15:11

The food that you eat is important. The exercises you do are helpful. Drinking plenty of water is good for you. But God says there's something even more important.

When you read today's verse from Matthew 15, did you catch what's more important? It's *what you think about.* When you spend time thinking about things God says won't help you, then you'll talk about things that God says cannot help you. This might cause other people to think about those things.

The impact of your words is bigger than a good breakfast and stronger than your most impressive muscles. It spreads further than a spilled glass of water. Choose what you think about carefully because it can lead to either helpful *or careless* conversations.

Thought choices lead to word choices, God. I want my thoughts to tell my mouth the good words I should say.

BREAKING DOWN THOUGHTS

We break down every thought and proud thing
that puts itself up against the wisdom of God.
2 CORINTHIANS 10:5

When people tell you something, do you believe it automatically or do you ask questions? They might be lying, they may be speaking gossip (things they aren't sure are true about others), or they might think they're telling you the truth. They might even be telling you the truth.

God's Word says you should break down the things you think about. Look at what you consider from all angles. Does what you think about sound different than what God says is true? If so, shift what you're thinking about. Is what you're thinking about unkind to someone? It's time to change your thinking. Does what you're thinking about challenge God? Time to drop the challenge. You cannot improve God's wisdom.

I should listen to You carefully, Lord.
I should also think with purpose and speak
with wisdom. Help me do all three.

THINKING THINGS

We take hold of every thought and make it obey Christ.
2 CORINTHIANS 10:5

Yesterday you read the first part of 2 Corinthians 10:5. Today you read the second half of this verse, and it's still talking about the importance of thinking for a boy like you.

If you have brothers, then maybe you like to wrestle. If you like to wrestle, then you probably want to win. If you want to win, then you will need to think about how you will do so. This is what it means to take hold of thoughts. You don't just let them do what they want; you give them house rules and enforce those rules.

Every thought that comes into your mind needs to obey Christ. You don't have to put up with thoughts that won't. God helps those who ask for help. That's true for the things you need to do. It's also true for the things you need to think about.

. . . .

Give me the wisdom to wrestle thoughts until they're willing to follow You, Lord. Don't let me give them a reason to convince me to make a bad choice.

HEAVENLY THOUGHTS

Keep your minds thinking about things in heaven.
Do not think about things on the earth.
COLOSSIANS 3:2

Your mind is a wonderful thing. You can use it to learn, imagine, and make decisions. But as a Christian, the Bible says to think about the right things. You can accept a new thought without question, or you can refuse to believe it. You already know that God wants you to believe His truth. So it's important to know what His Word says. It's the only way to understand truth.

You might have friends at school who don't know God, so they will think and talk about things that don't matter. But you know better. You can think about many things that will never help you but thinking about God and heaven—the place where you will live forever—is important. If you spend time thinking about "God things," then you won't have much time to think about things that will never help you.

I need to think wisely, God. Help me understand how to make good choices.

GOOD THOUGHTS

Their minds were sinful and they wanted
only to do things they should not do.
ROMANS 1:28

You've read about the need to do something with your thoughts that's different than just letting your mind think what it wants. Romans 1:28 talks about people who chose not to let God help them think. They did "things they should not do." That is what happens when you aren't careful with your thoughts. Your mind can convince you to do things you know are wrong.

Don't let your mind go wherever it wants. It will take you to places you don't belong. Don't do what you "should not do." Instead, follow God, even when none of your friends do. Concentrating on His thoughts will help you make good choices.

. . . .

I want to think good thoughts, Father. I want to make good choices. I want You to be pleased with the things I do. Keep my mind thinking about You and how You're always ready to help me.

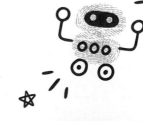

TURN FROM SIN

*Jesus. . .said, "Be sorry for your
sins and turn from them."*
MATTHEW 4:17

Dark and unwelcome thoughts lead to bad decisions. And once you begin making bad decisions, it can feel like you can't stop. But you can. God offers forgiveness when you admit you were wrong. He offers love for all people (even when they make bad choices), and He even said that by using your mind, you can choose to be sorry for your bad choice (sin) and then turn away from making that choice again.

Your mind doesn't have to think bad thoughts. You don't have to entertain thoughts that aren't welcome. God can help you ask them to leave. Sometimes the best way to do that is to read the Bible and other good Christian books. When your mind is on God, there isn't much room for unwelcome thoughts.

Thank You for giving me good things to think about, Lord. I need to remember that when bad thoughts come, I should think about You and all the help You give me.

THE ONLY IMPORTANT PERSON

For as he thinks in his heart, so is he.
PROVERBS 23:7

Whatever a boy thinks about, he becomes. If you make it a habit of thinking about taking something that doesn't belong to you, then eventually you will take it. That makes you a thief. But if you think a lot about ways to serve God, you will follow through. That will make you a servant of God.

Today's verse is about a man who thinks about things other than God. And it comes with a warning: "Do not eat the bread of a man who thinks only about himself. Do not have a desire for his fine food" (Proverbs 23:6). Why? Because he only thinks about what he wants and never thinks of anyone else. He isn't willing to help others, listen to them, or ask God to help them.

. . . .

When I think only of myself, I don't have room for anyone else, God. I don't have room for others, and I don't have room for You. Give my heart all the room it needs to welcome Your thoughts so I can do more of what You do.

LOVE GOD WITH EVERYTHING YOU'VE GOT

"Love the Lord your God with all your heart and with all your soul and with all your mind."
MATTHEW 22:37

Think about your favorite hobby. Maybe it's football or soccer. Or maybe it's video games. You think about that activity when you are at school or anywhere else. You can't wait to get out of school to play your favorite sport or to take advantage of your screen time.

Now think about the people you love the most. That could be parents or grandparents, brothers or sisters, or friends. There isn't much you wouldn't do for them. You can't imagine life without them. You may not always love them perfectly, but you choose to love them, and they have chosen to love you.

God already loves you. He made that choice before He even created the earth. Do you love Him? Do you think about him as much as you think about the people and hobbies you love? If not, make today's verse your prayer for the day.

God, help me to love You with all my heart, soul, and mind today.

HONORABLE THINKING

*God bought you with a great price. So honor
God with your body. You belong to Him.*
1 CORINTHIANS 6:20

The price God paid for you was the life of His Son, Jesus. He lived like you've lived. He grew like you're growing. And His perfect life was the only sacrifice God could accept to pay what it costs for you to break His rules. This is a very special gift and a gift that God offers to everyone willing to accept it.

God designed your body to see, touch, taste, smell, and hear. In addition to those five senses, He also gave you a mind so you can think. Because God bought you with a great price, you can use your mind to bring honor to God by following His commands. And you can use your five senses to honor God by appreciating God's beauty, by listening to sermons, or by enjoying the Lord's supper, also called "communion."

- -

*When I think about all You have done,
Lord, I'm so thankful. I want to honor You
with my thoughts and senses.*

GROWING UP

*When I was a child, I spoke like a child. I thought
like a child. I understood like a child. Now I am
a man. I do not act like a child anymore.*
1 CORINTHIANS 13:11

You're young, but you're growing up. You may not think of yourself as a child, but you're not really a grown up yet. That will come in time. It won't be that long, really.

Sometimes people will accept God's offer of rescue from their sin, but they want to stay like children. They don't want to grow up. They don't want to learn. They don't want to understand what God wants them to do.

This might happen when you stop thinking about the way God can help you grow up. After all, if you don't know what God wants, then you won't feel like you need to do anything more than what you're doing right now.

The *you* God made you to be is someone who grows up in the faith and thinks godly thoughts.

*I want to grow up with You, God.
I want to think godly thoughts.*

FEELINGS VS. FACTS

The way of a fool is right in his own eyes,
but a wise man listens to good teaching.
PROVERBS 12:15

When you're sick, an adult will ask you how you're feeling. They do this to see if you feel sick or well and not so much whether you feel sad or happy. A friend might be interested in knowing what kind of emotion you're experiencing. They might ask, "Why are you so mad?" or "What's making you smile so much today?"

Proverbs 12:15 suggests a foolish person pays more attention to feelings and a wise man pays more attention to facts. How do we know this? Well, the foolish man does what he wants because it makes him feel better. A wise man listens to good teaching because he wants to know the truth—no matter how he may feel.

. . . .

Thank You for providing good teaching, Father.
By listening and obeying it, I can become
wise in Your eyes, rather than my own.

DON'T MAKE THIS CHOICE

When I am afraid, I will trust in You.
PSALM 56:3

Do you ever get worried? You probably have. Did you know worrying is a choice? When you're afraid, you might think it makes sense to choose to worry. When you feel like you don't know what could happen, you might worry. When you wonder what other people think of you, you might choose to worry.

God doesn't want your feelings to cause you to make this choice. When you're afraid, don't know what might happen, or wonder what people think about you, take these feelings to God instead of choosing to worry.

God fears nothing, He knows what will happen every moment of every day, and He loves you no matter what anyone else thinks—plus, He's always with you. Pray and be thankful. He is a personal God who cares about what happens to you. You don't need to worry.

I admit that I sometimes choose worry, Lord. I want Your better choice. I want to trust You more than I rely on my own understanding.

TRUE PEACE

The peace of God is much greater than the human mind can understand. This peace will keep your hearts and minds through Christ Jesus.

PHILIPPIANS 4:7

God's peace is a gift you get to choose. As you do, you will feel calm, happy, and satisfied. And peace from God is greater and more wonderful than your mind can understand. It might even seem unbelievable. But it's true—and available. This peace can help you focus your thinking.

Instead of worrying, God's peace allows you to think without being distracted. God's peace can and will make life better. Instead of being afraid, you can believe God will take care of you. Instead of not knowing what will happen in the future, you can be satisfied, knowing that God has it all figured out. Instead of spending time wondering what people think of you, you can be happy, knowing God loves you.

. . . .

Good choices bring better feelings, God. Your peace changes how I feel.

STRONG FEELINGS

Then Jesus cried.
JOHN 11:35

Feelings are not your enemy. God created you to have feelings, and He gave them to you for a reason. When something hurts, you might feel sad. When you receive a birthday gift, you will feel happy. When you want to learn more about something, you will feel curious.

Ecclesiastes 3:4 says, "There is a time to cry, and a time to laugh; a time to have sorrow, and a time to dance."

When Lazarus died, Jesus cried. He knew He would raise Him from the dead soon, but He still felt the loss, so He wept.

Psalm 144 is a song of thanks. Here's how it describes God's people as He provides for them: "Happy are the people who have all this. Yes, happy are the people whose God is the Lord!" (verse 15).

Your feelings are natural and God-given but don't allow them to make decisions for you.

Thank You for never making me feel guilty for having feelings, Father. Teach me what to do with feelings when they come and then trust You with each next step.

NO FEAR

*"Be strong and have strength of heart!
Do not be afraid or lose faith. For the Lord
your God is with you anywhere you go."*
JOSHUA 1:9

Joshua was given a huge job. God wanted him to lead the people of Israel to the promised land. The people were afraid, and that fear kept them from their move-in day. They allowed how they felt to stop them from accepting something God had promised them.

Fear is a powerful feeling and often stops people from doing good things. That may be why Joshua told the people to "Be strong and have strength of heart" (Joshua 10:25). God wanted them to send fear away and keep faith nearby. That should be easy because God said He was close.

Joshua believed God. He was willing to invite feelings like amazement, eagerness, and excitement. They were great replacements for gloom, sadness, and anger.

Believe God and accept the feelings that show up when you go where He leads. He promises to be there.

. . . .

***Give me the strength to walk with You, Lord.
I believe You will go with me wherever I go.***

FEELINGS ARE NOT FOREVER

The Lord is near to those who have a broken heart.
PSALM 34:18

When you have feelings you don't want, feelings that are not helping, then you should know something: "The Lord is near to those who have a broken heart."

Feelings are not forever. No matter how bad you feel at any moment, God hasn't changed what He thinks about you. When your feelings want you to believe there's no way out of the bad things you experience, God whispers. "I am the Way and the Truth and the Life" (see John 14:6). God's way, truth, and life have always been available to those with a broken heart.

Don't fall for the lie that God doesn't care about your problems or heartache. He is near to you.

. . . .

I don't always feel like I matter, God, but You're waiting for me to talk to You. Here I am talking. You've done great things for me when I didn't know what to do. Thank You for being near to me, even when I don't feel like that's true.

ALWAYS IN CONTROL

*The Lord is full of loving-pity and kindness. He is
slow to anger and has much loving-kindness.*
PSALM 103:8

Do you ever wonder if God has feelings? Well, three days
ago, you read that Jesus wept. You read yesterday that
God stays close to the brokenhearted. God is described in
the Bible on a few occasions as angry, and Jesus got angry
too. But God often chooses love over anger, and kindness
before justice.

Yes, God has feelings, but the choices He makes are
always based on facts and always for your good. God
is always in control of how He feels. That's important to
remember the next time you want to get even with someone who is not kind.

Your feelings are important. They matter. But they are
never more important than the rules God gave you to live by.

. . . .

*It's easy to get so angry that I make bad decisions,
Father. I don't want my feelings to make my
choices. I can do things because You say they're
the right thing to do. Help me with this.*

BOATS, WAVES, AND WISDOM

Children are like boats thrown up and down on big waves. They are blown with the wind.

EPHESIANS 4:14

The verse you just read talks about people who were trying to get others to believe lies. It seems like these people were very convincing.

You might think it would be hard for anyone to trick you. You might even be right, but sometimes people are tricked into believing something because what they heard made them *feel* something. Paul said this experience is a bit like children who are like boats being tossed around by the wind and waves. You're not sure where you're going, and your feelings keep changing your direction.

Growing up means asking God to help you learn what things are true and what things are just stories. And one of the best ways you can do that is to read and study your Bible. It's the source of truth.

I feel good when I know Your truth, Lord. I feel cheated when I believe a lie. I want to know Your truth.

DON'T STAY ANGRY

A man's anger does not allow him to be right with God.
JAMES 1:20

It's not a sin to be angry. However, it's never helpful to *stay* angry.

You can be mad about the way a bully treats someone, but if you stay mad, you might end up doing the same thing—or something even worse.

The feeling of anger is powerful because it makes you want the others pay for doing the wrong thing. If they seem to be getting away with bad behavior, you no longer think mercy, kindness, and love are good gifts to give them. You might want to see them punished. But anger isn't helpful.

You can't easily follow God when He wants to show mercy and you want to hurt someone. As today's verse says, your anger does not allow you to be right with God.

. . . .

Keep me from staying angry, God. You want me to recognize when bad things happen, but You never want me to punish other people.

THE UNHAPPY MESSENGER

Jonah was not pleased at all, and he became angry.
JONAH 4:1

Jonah was a messenger. God wanted Jonah to share His message with the people who lived in Nineveh. They were doing the wrong thing and needed to stop. But Jonah didn't want to deliver this message. He didn't like the people of Nineveh, and he wanted to see them punished. But that wasn't what God wanted.

Once Jonah shared the message, they agreed that they had been doing the wrong thing and they wanted to stop. That didn't make Jonah happy either.

What can you learn from this? You were created to be a messenger of God—someone who tells others that Jesus died to save them from their sins. And yes, that means telling people you might not like about Jesus. You don't have the right to be angry about people becoming Christians.

I want to tell others about how Jesus can save them—even those who I don't like. Change my heart toward them, Lord.

GOD IS YOUR SAFE PLACE

My heart was troubled and I was hurt inside.
PSALM 73:21

Feelings can seem real, and what you feel can cause damage inside. It can make you think things that aren't true. It can make you consider doing things that you'd never think of doing if only you *felt* differently.

The writer of Psalm 73 felt troubled and hurt inside. Do you know how he overcame this? He made sure he was close to God. "As for me," he wrote, "it is good to be near God. I have made the Lord God my safe place" (Psalm 73:28).

How can you do this when you feel troubled or hurt inside? Prayer is one good way. Worship is another. You don't have to wait until Sunday to do either one. You can pray and worship anywhere. When you do, you will feel God's presence and feel safe.

. . . .

Lord, sometimes when I feel down, I pull away from everyone, even You. Remind me to turn to You when I'm upset. You are a safe place for me.

NO PITY PARTIES ALLOWED

*Ahab lay down on his bed and turned
his face away and would not eat.*
1 KINGS 21:4

Since Ahab was the king, he was used to getting everything he wanted—and he wanted a lot. Ahab visited a vineyard one day, and it was pleasant and refreshing. The grapes were excellent. That's when the king decided he wanted to own the vineyard. Someone else had done all the work but Ahab wanted it. When the owner refused to sell it to him, he had a big pity party.

You aren't a king, but you've probably wanted something that belonged to someone else. Maybe you offered to trade something for it or give them your allowance, but he didn't want to sell it. How did you respond? Like Ahab who was selfish? Or like Jesus who never did anything out of selfishness?

Help me make good choices, God, when I want something. When I start to act like Ahab, remind me that Jesus lives inside me and will empower me to let go of what I want.

98

GIVE HIM YOUR WORRIES

Give all your worries to Him because He cares for you.
1 PETER 5:7

How did you feel the last time you told your best friend about your worries? It helped a little, didn't it? Today's verse has an even better idea—give all your worries to God because He cares for you. This verse is a lot like Psalm 55:22: "Give all your cares to the Lord and He will give you strength. He will never let those who are right with Him be shaken."

God will listen to you, comfort you, give you strength, and take care of you. How well does He know you? He even knows how many hairs you have on your head right now (see Matthew 10:30). He takes care of His creation, but He also died for you. He loves you that much. Give Him your worries in prayer. He'll gladly take them from you.

* * *

Lord, thank You for loving me so much that You'll even take my worries from me. Remind me to give them to You instead of trying to solve them myself.

PRAY ABOUT EVERYTHING

Do not worry. Learn to pray about everything.
Give thanks to God as you ask Him for what you need.
PHILIPPIANS 4:6

For the next couple of weeks, you'll read about why the *you* God created needs to be in contact with the God who created you. This connection is prayer.

Not praying is kind of like saying, "God made me. He knows how to help me. He knows what I can be someday, but I think I'll do what I want instead." Today's verse says to pray about *everything.* Don't choose your close friends without praying. Don't try to do your homework without praying. Don't play sports or anything else without praying.

As you ask Him for what you need, give thanks to God. It leads to peace, as Philippians 4:7 says: "The peace of God is much greater than the human mind can understand. This peace will keep your hearts and minds through Christ Jesus."

There's nothing off limits in my prayer to You, Lord. Thank You! Help and teach me to stop worrying. You want to hear from me. Help me to want to hear from You.

SIMPLE PRAYERS

"When you pray, do not say the same thing over and over again making long prayers like the people who do not know God. They think they are heard because their prayers are long."
MATTHEW 6:7

If you think prayer is hard, then you might think you need to learn certain words or ways to say something to impress God. Matthew 6 indicates that you can say what you need to say in a way that makes sense to you. God understands. You don't need a secret dictionary with words that only good Christians use. You can say what's on your heart with a good God.

Some people who pray will say a lot of words. Those who hear it might not even know what they mean. God will listen to any kind of prayer, but He is happy when guys like you talk to Him like you're talking to a friend.

· ·

Hello, God. I'm talking to You because I want to be closer to You. Thanks for taking care of me. Let's do this again soon.

OPEN COMMUNICATION

Never stop praying.
1 THESSALONIANS 5:17

You talk to people, right? You don't make an appointment to speak to them. You just say what's on your heart. When you think about praying to God, He doesn't make you check in with His staff to find a good time to talk. He's available any time, any place, for any reason. Pray, and keep praying. Speak, and keep speaking. Wonder, and keep asking.

God created you to be in a relationship with Him. Part of being in a relationship is conversation. You started talking to God the minute you asked Him to save you from your sin, and the conversation continues to this day. He never takes a vacation from you. When you need help, He's there, so there's never a time when you shouldn't pray. Even if you mess up and sin, confess it right away. God is quick to forgive.

· ·

I love the fact that You didn't place restrictions on prayer, Father. I want to talk to You every day, all day.

CONVERSATION BETWEEN FRIENDS

[Jesus said,] "If you get your life from Me and My Words live in you, ask whatever you want."
JOHN 15:7

If you don't know God, then it can feel awkward if you try speaking to Him. It might feel like talking to a stranger. You don't know what's important to Him and don't feel comfortable talking about things that are bugging you.

In John 15:7, Jesus was reminding His friends that they got life from Him. They were learning what He had to say, so when they asked questions, they were friends who were asking a Friend to help them. Good friends know one another so well that they can ask each other whatever they want.

That's what it's like to talk to God. You learn all you can about Him so when you ask Him something, you know He can help you.

. . . .

I want to be Your friend, Lord. Thank You for being mine. And help me to know You well enough that I won't ask for things You have already said no to.

GREAT AND WONDERFUL THINGS

*[God said,] "Call to Me, and I will answer
you. And I will show you great and wonderful
things which you do not know."*
JEREMIAH 33:3

Do you have friends who don't answer the phone when you call them? Maybe the person you consider your best friend doesn't answer when you need him the most. You don't have to worry about that with God. He says, "Call to Me, and I will answer you." Not only that, but he will show you great and wonderful things.

King Solomon called out to God and God showed him great and wonderful things. He asked God for wisdom and understanding, and here's how God responded: "You have not asked for riches, or for the life of those who hate you. But you have asked for understanding to know what is right. Because you have asked this, I have done what you said. See, I have given you a wise and understanding heart. No one has been like you before, and there will be no one like you in the future" (1 Kings 3:11–13).

God would love to show you great and wonderful things too. Just ask.

Show me great and wonderful things, God!

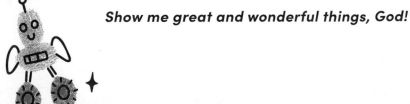

TIRED PRAYERS

"Watch and pray so that you will not be tempted. Man's spirit is willing, but the body does not have the power to do it."
MATTHEW 26:41

Today's verse is part of the story of Jesus. It wouldn't be long before Jesus would die on the cross. Just before that happened, some of His followers joined Him to pray. The problem? Well, they kept falling asleep. Jesus prayed and His followers kept taking naps.

It probably seems easy to say that you would never do that, but you might have fallen asleep while praying before. The good news? God doesn't punish people who get sleepy when they pray. But He does say prayer can keep you from being tempted to do wrong things. You may really want to talk to God, but you may not have the strength to pray for very long. God wants you to ask Him for help, especially when you feel tired and weak.

Sometimes, I can't seem to tell You much before I fall asleep, Father. But keep me awake long enough to say the important stuff. I know it gives me the spiritual strength to resist sin.

SELFLESS PRAYERS

Pray for the things that are needed.
You must watch and keep on praying.
Remember to pray for all Christians.
EPHESIANS 6:18

There's a story of a lady who owned a notebook with all the names of the people in her church. She would read through that list every day and pray for every single person. That probably took a lot of time but think about how you would feel if you were on her list. And think about the spiritual blessings you might receive from that.

You might want to start your own notebook and as you hear each person at your church tell you about things they need, write it down and begin praying for it. But don't stop there. Pray for their spiritual growth and that God would use them to tell others about Jesus. They can reach people you will never meet.

I want to think of other people when I pray, Lord.
I want to include the things they need when I spend
time talking with You. And remind me to pray for
their spiritual growth and their spiritual influence.

WHEN TROUBLE COMES

*Do not give up when trouble comes. Do not
let anything stop you from praying.*
ROMANS 12:12

Trouble is going to show up. It doesn't even need an invitation. It never asks if you want it hanging around. It doesn't care if you're too busy. It doesn't say it's sorry—because it's *not* sorry.

Trouble wants you to give up. It wants you to fear the future. Trouble likes to be a bully and hopes that you give it everything it wants. It will ask for your time, attention, and thoughts. It doesn't want you to think of anything else but what it has to say. Trouble wants to be the most important thing in your life.

It doesn't have to be. God doesn't want it to be. God can easily solve trouble—and He wants you to let Him. When trouble comes, talk to God, and stop listening to trouble. Trouble rarely speaks truth. . .God always does.

- -

*Trouble seems big and important, God.
It wants me to pay attention, and I usually
do. Help me to remember that when trouble
comes, You've already got a plan.*

THE LORD IS NEAR

The Lord is near to all who call on Him,
to all who call on Him in truth.
PSALM 145:18

Do you pray because someone told you that you should? That's a pretty good reason. But what if there's a more important reason to pray? There is, you know.

Prayer is more than nice words spoken *about* God at special times. Prayer is a conversation *with* God about the things you're concerned about. Yes, you should let God know how much He means to you. This is important. But God also wants to know what you struggle with. He wants to know why you struggle. He wants to listen to you when you hurt.

So pray—not because you have to but because you get to. When you pray, you have God's attention. Be truthful in all you say to Him. Know that what you say to Him is private. Remember that God loves you and wants you to know Him.

It's a gift to have Your attention, Father.
When I speak, You listen. When I hurt,
You help. When I cry, You comfort.

FORGIVENESS IS HARD

"Love those who hate you. (Respect and give thanks for those who say bad things to you. Do good to those who hate you.) Pray for those who do bad things to you and who make it hard for you."

MATTHEW 5:44

Maybe you think God doesn't know how much someone has hurt you. Why would He ask you to pray for those who do bad things to you? But He *does* ask. He knows it's hard. He allowed his only Son to be beaten and killed by people who mocked Him on the cross. As Jesus was near death, He asked the Father to forgive His killers because they didn't know what they were doing (Luke 23:34).

Nobody is so mean that God won't forgive them. The next time someone says bad things to you or about you, love that person enough to say a prayer for him. You never know. He might even become a Christian after you've prayed for him.

. . . .

Sometimes, I don't want to forgive, Lord. I want people who hurt me to know that they hurt me. Give me the courage and power to forgive them.

CALLED TO A MEETING

Let us go with complete trust to the throne of God.
We will receive His loving-kindness and have His
loving-favor to help us whenever we need it.
HEBREWS 4:16

Have you ever been called to the principal's office? Maybe your school is at home and a call to the principal's office could be a meeting with a parent. This kind of meeting usually means you've done something wrong. So you don't look forward to these meetings.

God is calling you to a meeting. But it's not for a lecture or a punishment. He tells the Christian to approach Him on His throne with complete trust. He wants to give us His kindness, love, and favor. Isn't that amazing? The God who created the universe wants to meet with *you*. Make sure you do that today.

I want to meet with You, God. I want to be
bold when I tell You what's going on in my life.
I want to listen when You speak to me.

GUILT-FREE

If we tell Him our sins, He is faithful and we
can depend on Him to forgive us of our sins.
He will make our lives clean from all sin.

1 JOHN 1:9

You've read that God wants to forgive you. You need to be forgiven for breaking His rules. How does that work? 1 John 1:9 is a great answer.

Some Bibles use the word *confess* when it comes to the rules we break. This just means that you tell God about the rules you break and admit you were wrong to break them. Read today's verse again. Does it say that God gets mad and tries to punish you? It actually says God can be trusted to take the things you share and turn the truth into an opportunity to forgive you and make you clean. God erases your guilt and looks at you as someone who is guilt-free.

* *

I want to be guilt-free, Father. I want
to tell You what I did wrong so You can
forgive me and clean my record.

DON'T STOP LOOKING

"Look to the Lord and ask for His strength. Look to Him all the time."
1 CHRONICLES 16:11

If you need another reminder that God wants to help you, today's verse is the one. *Looking to God* means you admire Him. *Asking for His strength* means you believe He will help. And *all the time* means these things are as natural as breathing.

Nothing about coming to God is meant to be difficult or scary. It's like the joy you experience waiting to tell your mom about something good that happened, the arrival of a grandparent, or a visit from your best friend. You can look forward to every visit with God.

The words you say don't just float around an empty room. The same God who made the earth, sky, and sea is with you when you speak His name. He pays attention. He notices who you pray for. He knows how He'll help you.

I'm here for another visit, Lord. Thanks for listening.

ASK

*You want something but cannot get it,
so you fight for it. You do not get things
because you do not ask for them.*

JAMES 4:2

Your friends might have the newest video game, phone, or sneakers. Maybe you've asked your parents for those things, and they told you to wait a little longer. Christian families have different priorities than the rest of the world, so your parents might want to give more money at church or to a homeless shelter instead. You don't always need the newest toys or clothes, anyway. But when you do ask your parents for something you need, they usually provide it, right?

God wants you to ask for the things you believe you need. In fact, today's verse says sometimes you don't get things because you didn't ask Him for them. So go ahead and ask him. You can count on Him to give you exactly what you need.

When I refuse to ask You for things, God, then the answer will always be no. Remind me to ask.

BELIEVE IT TO SEE IT

*Our life is lived by faith. We do not live
by what we see in front of us.*
2 CORINTHIANS 5:7

If you want to see really small things, you need to use a microscope. These small things exist; you just need to find the right way to see them. If you want to look at planets, you need to use a telescope to see things that are very far away. If you want to see what God is doing, you have to live by faith.

Galatians 2:20 explains what living by faith means: "I have been put up on the cross to die with Christ. I no longer live. Christ lives in me. The life I now live in this body, I live by putting my trust in the Son of God. He was the One Who loved me and gave Himself for me."

There are things that only those who follow God can understand. In the Christian life, you have to believe before you can see spiritual truth. Only after you believe does God allow you to see what He's doing.

. . . .

*Increase my trust in You, Father,
so that I can live by faith.*

TRUST THE WORD

*As for God, His way is perfect. The Word
of the Lord has stood the test.*
PSALM 18:30

Depending on the sources, somewhere between 400,000 and one million books are published every year. That's a lot of books! And many of them have helpful things to say. But King Solomon offered this advice: "There is no end to the writing of many books and reading many of them makes the body tired" (Ecclesiastes 12:12). As a young boy, the best book you can read is the Bible. It has stood the test of time.

Maybe you have been asking God for guidance about something but couldn't hear His voice. If so, ask yourself whether you are seeking truth in the Bible. Then ask yourself if you agree with what you are reading in His Word. If God gives you a rule you don't want to obey, then He may stop showing you what to do next. His way is perfect, no matter how hard it might seem.

. . . .

*Help me remember that walking with You means
doing what You say, Lord. Help me obey Your Word.*

THE IMPORTANCE OF OTHERS

What does the Lord ask of you but to do what is fair and to love kindness, and to walk without pride with your God?
MICAH 6:8

If you've been successful at something at school, others will tell you how good you are. That can lead to a prideful heart. You'll know you have one when you start thinking other people are less important than you are. If that's the case, then it's time to listen to the apostle Paul: "Nothing should be done because of pride or thinking about yourself. Think of other people as more important than yourself. Do not always be thinking about your own plans only. Be happy to know what other people are doing" (Philippians 2:3–4).

Today's verse says God asks you to be fair, to love kindness, and to walk without pride. If you sense that you haven't been doing these things, stop right now and ask God for forgiveness.

I don't want to be so filled with pride that I can't walk with You, God. Help me to be nice, kind, and respectful.

PAID IN FULL

"Walk in all the way the Lord your God has told you. Then you may live, it may be well with you."
DEUTERONOMY 5:33

Breaking God's rules comes with a death sentence. That's a pretty big fine, but the good news is that Jesus paid your fine before you were ever born. You just have to accept the terms that come with the cancelation of the penalty. You have to believe that Jesus exists, died in your place for the sins you committed, rose from the dead, and returned to heaven to be with God the Father.

It's still important to obey God's rules. After all, God didn't just give instructions for life because He thought it would be fun. He knows that agreeing to obey will help you follow Him. Why is this important? Obedience leads to a fulfilling life—one in which you'll know much better how to handle things that come up.

* * *

My walk with You, Father, will take me through hard places, but You are with me leading the way. This walk has a finish line and that's with You. Thank you for canceling the penalty of my sin. I plan to keep walking with You.

TAKE ANOTHER STEP

Your Word is a lamp to my feet and a light to my path.
PSALM 119:105

Your walk with God isn't without hazards. Today's verse shows that God knows where you are, though, and how to get you to where you need to be.

When you read the verse, you almost get the picture of someone walking in the dark in a place where he has never been. He doesn't know if he's about to run into a tree or walk off a cliff. God's promise to this adventurer, and to you, is that He will make sure this person can see far enough to take another step. When you read God's Word, you get just enough information to take another step in your journey. Keep reading because that helps you take the step after that.

When I go on vacation, I want to know what I'll do, Lord. Help me understand my journey with You is more amazing than any vacation I'll ever take. And You're my personal guide.

SHEEP FOLLOW

[God] has made us to belong to Christ Jesus so we can work for Him. He planned that we should do this.
EPHESIANS 2:10

The Bible says people who follow God are like sheep. Maybe that's because we need someone to follow who knows more than we do. Maybe it's because, without a shepherd, we would get lost.

Ephesians 2:10 tells you *why you were made.* God made you to follow Jesus and to do what He says needs to be done. This has always been God's plan. It was His plan before you were born, and it's His plan today.

The *you* God made you to be is a young man who is satisfied in knowing God and willing to follow Him all the days that you live. This journey may not always be smooth or easy. There may be hard things that you'll need to face, but you never face any of them alone.

. . . .

Lord, thank You for creating me to follow Jesus. Lead and guide me in the work You want me to do for Your kingdom.

DON'T FOLLOW YOUR HEART

Let the Holy Spirit lead you in each step.
Then you will not please your sinful old selves.
GALATIANS 5:16

You've probably heard people tell you to follow your heart. But the Bible doesn't teach that. In fact, it says, "The heart is fooled more than anything else, and is very sinful. Who can know how bad it is?" (Jeremiah 17:9). And God's Word says, "Trust in the Lord with all your heart, and do not trust in your own understanding. Agree with Him in all your ways, and He will make your paths straight" (Proverbs 3:5–6).

When you go through life not walking with God, you'll always wind up doing the wrong thing. Your way of thinking apart from God leads you far from Him. Proverbs 3 says *not* to trust in your own understanding. And today's verse from Galatians says to let *the Holy Spirit* guide your life. That's the only way to make sure your old way of thinking doesn't influence what steps you'll take today.

Remind me that nothing good happens when I step off Your path, Lord. Lead and guide me because I need Your direction.

THERE ALL ALONG

Come close to God and He will come close to you.
JAMES 4:8

A few days ago, you read Psalm 119:105. If you've forgotten the verse, read it again: "Your Word is a lamp to my feet and a light to my path." Now, read James 4:8 again: "Come close to God and He will come close to you."

Today's verse isn't saying that God's presence only happens if you stay close. God never leaves or abandons you. But if you haven't been following Him, then you won't realize how close He is. When you do follow Him (come close) by taking a step in His direction, then you'll see that He's there. He's always been there.

You were always made to follow God. The light that He gives you helps you recognize Him when you're looking somewhere else.

. . . .

Sometimes I get confused and think You're not there, Lord. Remind me that I need to follow You to see that You're with me.

RUNNING THE RACE WELL

*Let us put every thing out of our lives that keeps us
from doing what we should. Let us keep running
in the race that God has planned for us.*

HEBREWS 12:1

What do you have that you don't need? What do you own
that keeps you from following God? Lots of things can keep
you from God, but you really like some of those things.
Getting rid of them can seem like a punishment.

Imagine yourself in a race and you make the choice
to carry all the things you enjoy with you as you run. You
might have a video game controller, a sports bag, and
maybe a TV in a pack strapped over your shoulder. Would
that make it easier or harder to run?

There's a reason these things need to have less importance than God. Don't get attached to things that can keep
you away from living the way He wants.

- -

*I need to always run toward You, God.
I don't want to try to carry stuff I don't
need. Help me make better choices.*

BE LIKE JESUS

The one who says he belongs to Christ should
live the same kind of life Christ lived.
1 JOHN 2:6

When people look at you, they should see Jesus. When they see what you say and do, they should see examples of the things Jesus said and did.

People don't expect someone who follows Jesus to be rude and unkind. They wouldn't expect a Christian to tell stories about other people that aren't true. They wouldn't expect him to be a bully.

No human can ever be a perfect mirror all the time, but 1 John 2:6 says that if you belong to Jesus, then you should live a life that looks like His. When you don't, find out why. And ask God the Father to help your life look more like His Son's life.

. . . .

Father, there are times when the choices I make
don't really look like choices Jesus would make.
I want to learn more so I can be more like Him.

THE FOOTSTEPS OF GOD

"I will walk among you and be your God."
LEVITICUS 26:12

You may remember that God doesn't leave or abandon you. He doesn't deny that He knows you. His love for you is well known. But this verse says God will walk among you and He will be your God.

He's not embarrassed by you. He'll stick with you even when you break His rules again. This is what he said to the people of Israel. He also said it so you would know the kind of God He is.

God loves you, lives with you, and you can learn from Him. He never leaves, even when you forget that He walks with you everywhere you go. God's footsteps show up on the path He asks you to walk because He's right there with you.

* * *

Because I can't see You, Lord, I sometimes feel like I'm alone. Thank you for this reminder that we're partners in this journey. You and I are friends on a walk.

ACCESS TO LIGHT

Jesus spoke to all the people, saying, "I am the Light of the world. Anyone who follows Me will not walk in darkness. He will have the Light of Life."
JOHN 8:12

Everything you need to see in order to walk with God comes from God. He's given you spiritual eyes, a mind to understand, and "light" to help everything to make sense.

God doesn't send you to a deep and dark cave and then instruct you to find your own way out. He knows the way through every difficult place. Psalm 23:4 suggests that you can say, "I will not be afraid of anything, because You are with me."

If you were to live in a world that had no light, it would be easy to give up. It would be hard to have hope. Thank God that you have access to light, life, and love. All three come from God—and He wants you to see them.

. . . .

May my heart long for Your light, God. May I see where to go because I spend time with You.

STRONG AGAIN

*He makes me strong again. He leads
me in the way of living right with Himself
which brings honor to His name*
PSALM 23:3

At some point in your life, you will feel the need to rest. Your muscles might get sore, and you might feel sick. Or you might feel emotionally tired. God's promise to you is that He can make you strong, and He wants to lead you. That's big news. You never have to walk alone. God doesn't run ahead to see if you can catch up. He doesn't try to make things hard for you.

Walk with Him, make good choices with His help, and honor His name. As you do, you'll find hope. You'll also find joy in the Lord. And you'll experience peace in knowing Jesus.

. . . .

*Never, ever, not even once will I have to
struggle alone, Father. Give me the courage
to walk and the strength to keep walking.
Help me make choices that honor You.*

KNOWING JESUS

*Learn to know our Lord Jesus Christ
better. He is the One Who saves.*
2 PETER 3:18

Would you like to know *about* Jesus, or would you rather *know* Jesus? There's a difference. If you know *about* Him, then you know facts about Him—like that He has always existed. But knowing Jesus means you have a relationship that goes beyond knowing the facts. It also means you know the one you're learning about.

The difference might be like knowing the year your mom was born, what color eyes she has, and where she grew up but never spending any time with her. You wouldn't know what she likes, how she does things, or how to make her happy.

You can know God personally and follow Him faithfully. As you do, you will know Jesus better.

- -

*I can know You, Lord, and I want to. Be my friend
and let me be Yours. Help me see who You are
by seeing what You do and how You care.*

THE BOOK TO KNOW

All the Holy Writings are God-given and are made alive by Him. Man is helped when he is taught God's Word. It shows what is wrong. It changes the way of a man's life. It shows him how to be right with God.
2 TIMOTHY 3:16

You may have heard adults talk about self-help books. Many who read them are really trying to improve their lives. And some of those books can be helpful. But today's verse reminds us that Christians are helped most when they are taught by God's Word. It not only shows us what is wrong, but it also changes the way we think and how to be right with God.

God's Word is different than anything you can read anywhere else. It contains spiritual power that no other book has. And it is eternal, as Isaiah 40:8 says: "The grass dries up. The flower loses its color. But the Word of our God stands forever."

I want to read Your Word, God. There's so much to learn, and You have so much to teach. I need to know You better.

LIVING AND POWERFUL

*God's Word is living and powerful. . . . It tells what
the heart is thinking about and what it wants to do.*
HEBREWS 4:12

Have you ever heard someone say the Bible is an old book that isn't important anymore? That person couldn't be more wrong. God says His Word is living and powerful and can tell you things about your thoughts and plans. Not only does the Bible help you understand God better, but it helps you know yourself better too.

How?

The Bible is *living* in the sense that the Holy Spirit takes what you read and plants it deep into your heart. He uses it to see if you are thinking and believing the right things. The Bible is *powerful* in the sense that it can change your heart and mind in an instant. There's never been a more important book. Make time to read it every day.

* * *

*I can understand who I am when I read
the Bible, Father. Help me to make
the Bible a priority every day.*

STAND AGAINST THE DEVIL

*Give yourselves to God. Stand against the
devil and he will run away from you.*

JAMES 4:7

Satan will try to convince you that God can't be trusted
and that His rules are made to be broken. Then as soon
as you break a rule, he accuses you of doing something
wrong. He wants you to feel worthless. And he wants you
to hide from God.

But this isn't how God does things. He cheers you on to
success. When you fail by sinning against Him (and we all
do), repent—give yourself to God. You'll experience His forgiveness, not His accusation. By doing so, you are standing
against the devil—and he will run away from you. But you
cannot beat Satan in your own strength. You must confess
your sin and rely on the power of the Holy Spirit.

*I want to know You, Lord. I don't want
to listen to the enemy. He lies about You
and he lies to me. When I sin, remind me to
confess it so the devil will run away.*

JESUS IS GOD

The Word (Christ) was in the beginning.
The Word was with God. The Word was God.
JOHN 1:1

In John 14:8, Philip said to Jesus, "Lord, show us the Father. That is all we ask." Jesus responded, in part, by saying, "Whoever has seen Me, has seen the Father" (verse 9). In other words, Jesus and the Father are one (as Jesus said in John 10:30).

Jesus didn't come to earth with a message that was different from anything God the Father said. He came to earth to introduce God's new agreement with all people that offered a rescue plan to all who broke His rules.

You were created to know God. You do that by knowing Jesus. And the best way to know Jesus is by studying the Bible.

. . . .

Father, thank You for allowing me to
know You through Jesus and Your Word.
It's amazing that You created me to know
the all-powerful Creator of the universe!

SEARCHING FOR GOD

*"I love those who love me, and those who look
for me with much desire will find me."*

PROVERBS 8:17

Have you ever lost something you loved? Maybe you lost an electronic device. How hard did you search for it? Did you look everywhere? Did you ask if anybody had seen it? Did you maybe even pray that God would help you find it?

Do you put that same time, energy, and effort into looking for and finding God? Want to take a test to find out the answer to that question? How do you feel about going to church every Sunday? Can you miss some Sundays without feeling a change in your spiritual life? How often do you pray? Can you go days without talking to God? Do you look forward to reading the Bible? Or can you go weeks without ever opening it?

If you love God, then you will look for Him with much desire.

*I'm interested in knowing You better,
Father. Help me be more curious.
Deepen my desire for You.*

STOP SINNING

The person who lives by the help of Christ does not keep on sinning. The person who keeps on sinning has not seen Him or has not known Him.

1 JOHN 3:6

God made you to know Him. And if you have believed in Jesus as your Lord and Savior, then the Holy Spirit lives inside you. He helps you to stop sinning. You'll never reach a point when you stop sinning completely, but you now have the power to say no to sin. A guy who loves God wants to please Him more than he wants to please himself. A boy who doesn't know Jesus, though, keeps sinning because he doesn't have any power to say no.

Want another test to find out?

If you don't think about God's rules or care much about breaking them, then it might mean you don't know Him very well. . .or at all. If you are not sure whether you know Jesus, then talk to a parent or your pastor and ask them to help.

. . . .

I want to live by the help of Jesus, Father. I do not want to keep sinning. When I became a Christian, You gave me the power to say no to sin. Thank you!

LOVES COMES FROM GOD

*Dear friends, let us love each other, because
love comes from God. Those who love are
God's children and they know God.*

1 JOHN 4:7

You might know someone at church or school who is hard
to love. He might sit in the corner quietly. He might be odd.
He might even be a little mean. Take a chance and get to
know him anyway. Show him the love of Jesus by reaching
out without expecting him to care in return. It might lead
to a friendship that changes his entire life and where he
will spend eternity.

Remember Romans 5:8? It says, "While we were still
sinners, Christ died for us." We didn't deserve that kind of
love. We will never deserve it. And we can never earn it. As a
Christian, you can love people who might be odd or mean
because that love comes from God, as today's verse says.

. . . .

*One of the great things about being loved by You,
God, is being able to love others in a godly way.
Help me to love people the way You love me.*

FAIR, GOOD, AND RIGHT

"But let him who speaks with pride speak about this, that he understands and knows Me, that I am the Lord who shows loving-kindness and does what is fair and right and good on earth. For I find joy in these things," says the Lord.

JEREMIAH 9:24

Sometimes people think God is angry with humanity and the only thing He wants to do is make life hard for us. These people might believe God isn't worth knowing because they think He doesn't put much value on human lives. But you've already learned how God finds great value in you. Since He loves you so much, He's not going anywhere. He wants the best for you, so He does "what is fair and right and good on earth."

Does that sound like a God who doesn't think you are worth much? No—the truth is exactly the opposite of that. To make the point even clearer, God says that being fair, doing the right thing, and showing the world who He is are the very things that bring Him joy.

. . . .

Father, I want to know You better. Help me remember that You're always fair, good, and right.

FINDING GOD

"You will look for Me and find Me,
when you look for Me with all your heart."
JEREMIAH 29:13

For the Christian, God isn't hard to find. But He can feel like He's a million miles away when we have an unconfessed sin in our lives. That's probably how the people of Judah felt when the Babylonians took them into captivity for seventy years due to their sin. But God had a plan for His people. They would return from captivity, and they would look for God with their whole heart. And they would find Him.

Remember the last time you did something wrong at home or school? Did you try to hide it from your parents or a teacher? You didn't feel close to them at that point, did you? Your sin made you feel far from them. It's the same way with God. He wants you to confess your sin right away. That will make you clean again so you can seek Him with your whole heart.

When I sin, Lord, I want to be quick to confess
it so You never seem far away from me.

NOTHING LESS

*"This is life that lasts forever. It is to know
You, the only true God, and to know
Jesus Christ Whom You have sent."*
JOHN 17:3

Maybe you've wondered what you're supposed to do with your life. You might think about what job you would like or whether you'll go to college. You could think about your future and whether you'll be a dad. You might even wonder what you'll do tomorrow.

God's Word says that the life God gives you "lasts forever." Does that change how you think about what you'll do? It should. Life has to be more than what video game you'll play with friends, how soon you have to do a homework assignment, or what you'll eat at your next meal.

Knowing God and His Son, Jesus, is exactly what you should do. Nothing less. Sure, you've read that before, but really important ideas are worth repeating. God wants *you* to know *Him*.

· ·

*God, it shouldn't surprise me that You aren't
like anyone I've ever met. I want to get to
know You, to love You, and to serve
You with my whole heart.*

A NEW MIND

*"For My thoughts are not your thoughts, and
My ways are not your ways," says the Lord.*
ISAIAH 55:8

Have you ever met people from another country? Do they eat the exact same foods you eat? Do they use the same exact words you use? Do they do everything exactly the way you would do? When you meet God, you should understand He will not do things the same way you do. That shouldn't be surprising, but most people think it is.

Don't expect God to change. The Bible says you are supposed to change as you surrender to God. The apostle Paul said it this way: "Do not act like the sinful people of the world. Let God change your life. First of all, let Him give you a new mind. Then you will know what God wants you to do. And the things you do will be good and pleasing and perfect" (Romans 12:2).

*When I want You to do things my way, help
me to remember that I wait for You, Lord.
Change my thoughts and give me a new mind.*

NOT DESTROYED

It is because of the Lord's loving-kindness that we are not destroyed for His loving-pity never ends. It is new every morning. He is so very faithful.
LAMENTATIONS 3:22–23

God's love for you means you can avoid destruction if your faith is in Christ. Is God saying that if He didn't love you, He would destroy you? That might make Him seem scary and unkind. Perhaps He means that even when people make bad decisions, His loving-kindness (and His ability to turn bad circumstances into good outcomes) prevents destruction.

The love God offers you is an everyday gift. That means the death of Jesus on the cross covers all your sins, even the ones you will commit today. He is faithful, even when we are not.

You were made to be loved—by God. His love prevents the destruction of humanity and offers us lasting hope. Everything you know about God begins by understanding that He loves you. He always has.

. . . .

I'm a young man who needs You, Lord. Your gift of salvation shows how much You Love me. And Your love is changing me.

BETTER THAN

My lips will praise You because Your
loving-kindness is better than life.
PSALM 63:3

Think about the best day you have ever experienced. Maybe it was a trip to Disney World or scoring the game-winning touchdown for your football team or getting the latest and greatest video game console before all your friends did. A few days later, though, you probably realized that your happiness didn't last. Something happened at home or school, and you forgot all about how good you felt.

Today's verse reminds you that God's love is better than anything you can name. In fact, it says it's better than life itself. What does that mean? It means you were made to experience God's love not only here but also for all eternity. Two hundred years from now, you'll be in heaven, praising God for loving you. That's so much better than scoring a game-winning touchdown.

Your love is better than any good thing that's ever happened to me, God. Thank You for thinking so much of me. My lips will praise You because your loving-kindness is better than life.

PEACE IN THE STRUGGLES

"The mountains may be taken away and the hills may shake, but My loving-kindness will not be taken from you. And My agreement of peace will not be shaken," says the Lord who has loving-pity on you.
ISAIAH 54:10

In the days of Noah, God sent flood waters to cover the earth. But He made a promise to humankind after that: "As I promised that the waters of Noah should not flood the earth again, so I have promised that I will not be angry with you or speak sharp words to you" (Isaiah 54:9). Natural disasters will still occur—things like earthquakes, hurricanes, and tornadoes—but God's love will not be taken from His people.

You were created in God's image (Genesis 1:26–27). How much more loving could He be than to do that? Yes, you will still experience hard things here on earth. But don't fear. As a follower of Jesus—who is the Prince of Peace—you now have peace with almighty God. You can have peace in your struggles. How amazing is that?

When things are hard here on earth, Father, remind me that I have peace with You because I believe in Jesus.

ALIVE IN CHRIST

You, O Lord, are a God full of love and pity. You are slow to anger and rich in loving-kindness and truth.
PSALM 86:15

This might surprise you, but God isn't waiting to catch you doing something wrong. He doesn't get angry quickly or want to punish you the second you sin. Ephesians 2:5 says, "Even when we were dead because of our sins, He made us alive by what Christ did for us. You have been saved from the punishment of sin by His loving-favor." Isn't that great news?

As today's verse says, God is slow to anger and rich in loving-kindness and truth. God sends compassion so He can show you He understands the struggles you face. He's patient because He knows learning His ways will take time. He's kind because He knows His kindness makes every other message He has for you seem like a text from a good friend. He created You to show compassion toward you.

Lord, I'm still learning how to follow You. Thank You for being slow to anger and so willing to offer me Your loving-kindness.

142

GOD SINGS

The Lord your God is with you, a Powerful One Who wins the battle. . . . With His love He will give you new life. He will have joy over you with loud singing.

ZEPHANIAH 3:17

Singing is a great way to express what's in your heart. That's one of the reasons we sing during worship. You might also sing along with the radio when your parents drive you somewhere. Or you might sing in your bedroom when you stream your favorite song. But have you ever thought about the God of the universe loving you so much that *He* sings over *you*?

Yes, God sings!

Whatever you are dealing with right now, He is there to help you. The same God who led Moses and the people of Israel through the wilderness, helped King David win battles, and gave Abraham a child when he was old also wants what's best for *you*.

. . . .

I'm amazed that You sing because of Your love for me. It helps me realize how much You love me. Thank You!

ADOPTION DAY

See what great love the Father has for us that He would call us His children. And that is what we are.
1 JOHN 3:1

Adoption is a beautiful thing. A child in need of a family becomes part of a family. How? Adoptive parents see that child and decide to give him a home. The child gets a new name and all the rights of a natural-born son.

When you accept Christ's offer of rescue from your sin, you become an adopted son of *God*. He wants and loves you. He places you in His family and calls you His child. Your new life in Christ will give you purpose and direction. And you'll never have to wonder whether He loves you. He does!

. . . .

You're my Father, and I'm Your son. You chose me, and I chose You. I want to become more comfortable in Your family. Thank You for being patient with me.

UNDERSTANDING GOD'S LOVE

*I pray that you will be able to understand how wide
and how long and how high and how deep His love is.*
EPHESIANS 3:18

Go west and just keep going. Go north as far as you possibly can. If you could travel in space to the farthest parts of the universe, God's love goes with you. You can't outrun it, escape it, or even make it go away. God's love simply waits for you to finally choose it. And why wouldn't you? It's more important than your greatest treasure.

When you sin, you might think that you disappoint God. But even then He never removes His love from you. When you want and need God's kindness, He'll give it to you. Then He asks you to share what He's given you because others need it just as much.

God's love makes you a partner with Him in sharing love, kindness, and mercy.

*Your love follows me wherever I go, Lord.
I want this love to change the way other people
see me—because they see You in me.*

HE GOES BEYOND

I pray that you will know the love of Christ.
His love goes beyond anything we can understand.
I pray that you will be filled with God Himself.
EPHESIANS 3:19

As you get older, you will realize how much your parents loved you. They do so much to provide a good life for you. Your dad or your mom (or both of them) work to pay for everything your family needs. They make decisions about your healthcare, and they are always looking for ways to keep you safe.

God loves you even better—in ways you will never understand. Psalm 91:11 says, "For He will tell His angels to care for you and keep you in all your ways." You won't see them, but they are always there. And 2 Corinthians 1:3–4 says, "We give thanks to the God and Father of our Lord Jesus Christ. He is our Father Who shows us loving-kindness and our God Who gives us comfort. He gives us comfort in all our troubles."

God, your Father, is always with you, especially in the hard times.

. . . .

Thank You for loving me in ways I will never understand, Lord. That is so encouraging.

GOD IS GOOD

O give thanks to the Lord, for He is good.
His loving-kindness lasts forever.
1 CHRONICLES 16:34

Do you have a grandmother or grandfather, or maybe an aunt or uncle who is good to you? Maybe that person remembers you on your birthday every single year. Or maybe that person gives you great advice about problems at school or with friends. Make sure to honor that that person.

Even if a guy is totally alone in this world, he still has God. And He is *always* good—His loving-kindness lasts forever. Think about ways God has been good to you. He has saved you from the penalty of your sin and given you a new life in Christ. He has provided for you in ways you probably never imagined. And He is always present in your life.

Give thanks to the Lord, for He is good!

. . . .

I want to honor You, Father. The work
You do in my life is amazing. Your love is
incredible, and I appreciate it so much.

NO COMPARISON

"O Lord, God of Israel, there is no God like You in heaven or on earth. You keep Your promises and show loving-kindness to Your servants who walk with You with all their hearts."
2 CHRONICLES 6:14

Do you remember the last time you had a substitute teacher at school? Or if you are home-schooled, maybe a friend's parent had to fill in as your teacher for a day when your parent was sick. That person did the best job possible, but it's hard to be a substitute. Especially since that person didn't know all the material your regular teacher planned to teach that day.

Thankfully, you never have to worry about that with God. There is no God like Him in heaven or on earth. No substitute can ever take His place. He's always present, always keeps His promises, and loves you more than any person ever could.

What better reason to walk with Him with all your heart?

Lord, there is no substitute or comparison for You. Empower me to walk with You with all my heart today.

GOD IS FOR YOU

Since God is for us, who can be against us?
ROMANS 8:31

Do you like to win? Whether you're on a robotics team, play baseball, or love chess, there is someone who is your biggest competitor. You might have lost against that person or team several times and can't figure out a way to win. In this life, you'll face people who are bigger, tougher, faster, and smarter than you. But Christians don't have to worry about that.

God is for you. He's never against you. Did you know that? Since God is for you, it doesn't matter who else is against you. If you are sharing the gospel with a friend and someone makes fun of you, that's okay. God is for you. If you are competing in a contest and someone is better than you, that's okay. Do your best for Jesus and represent Him well.

If God is for you, who could possibly hurt you?

Lord, knowing You are for me makes me feel calm. Help me to represent You well, even when the world stands against me.

HONOR GOD WITH YOUR BODY

*Christ lives in me. The life I now live in this body,
I live by putting my trust in the Son of God. He was
the One Who loved me and gave Himself for me.*

GALATIANS 2:20

You were given one body, and it will last as long as you live. It may be a good and strong body or maybe not. Either way, God didn't make a mistake. Keep in mind that Jesus—by God's Spirit—lives in you if you have placed your faith in Him.

Here's what the apostle Paul says about the Christian's body: "Do you not know that your body is a house of God where the Holy Spirit lives? God gave you His Holy Spirit. Now you belong to God. You do not belong to yourselves. God bought you with a great price. So honor God with your body. You belong to Him" (1 Corinthians 6:19–20).

Take good care of the body God gave you. It's a way to honor Him.

. . . .

*Heavenly Father, help me love You more
and be less concerned with how I look or
what I'm able to do. May I take excellent
care of the body You've given me.*

TRUE LOVE

*This is love! It is not that we loved God but
that He loved us. For God sent His Son to
pay for our sins with His own blood.*
1 JOHN 4:10

Before you were born, your parents loved you. They talked about you, bought a crib and clothes for you, and prayed for you. They thought about you all the time. When you arrived, you didn't know enough to love them. But over time you grew to love them.

This is a picture of the Christian life. Before you were born, God loved you. How do you know this? Today's verse says He sent His Son—His only Son—to pay for your sins with His own blood. If God loves you, then you know He loves His own Son. And you know how much pain it caused Him to watch His Son die on the cross for you. But He allowed that out of His great love for you.

. . . .

*Your love is free to me, Lord, but it was very
expensive for You. Thank You for sending Jesus
to prove how much You love me. Your choice
showed a love that no one can match.*

ALWAYS WITH YOU

Hope never makes us ashamed because the love of God has come into our hearts through the Holy Spirit Who was given to us.

ROMANS 5:5

You know that Jesus died on a cross to pay for our sins. You probably know that He came back to life three days later. But did you know that He lived on earth for another forty days before He went back to heaven? And that when He returned to heaven, He sent back His Holy Spirit to live in Christians?

When a boy like you decides to follow Jesus, the Holy Spirit makes His home inside you. He helps, teaches, and encourages you. And He gives you hope. Here's how the apostle Paul said it: "Our hope comes from God. May He fill you with joy and peace because of your trust in Him. May your hope grow stronger by the power of the Holy Spirit" (Romans 15:13).

If things don't always go your way (and they won't), you don't have to lose hope. Hope lives inside you.

I'm Your son, God. You love me. You give me a reason to hope, no matter how hard life gets.

YOU CAN TRUST GOD

Who can keep us away from the love of Christ?
Can trouble or problems? Can suffering wrong
from others or having no food? Can it be because
of no clothes or because of danger or war?
ROMANS 8:35

Once God gives you His love, He won't allow anyone to steal it. When trouble comes, God's love stays. When problems show up, you can still experience His love. No suffering can take God's love away. There's no disease or accident or fear or struggle that could take you away from His love. Nothing!

God's love is deep, high, and wide, and you can't run away from it. You can even try to avoid God's love, but it will keep following you. Why? Because you need God's love and He wants you to have it.

God's love makes you *you*.

. . . .

You take care of me because You love me, Father.
But when trouble comes, I will rely on Your love and
comfort because I know You will never leave me.

153

GOD KNOWS WHAT HE'S DOING

*Trust your work to the Lord, and your
plans will work out well.*
PROVERBS 16:3

Some people find today's verse confusing. They might think the Bible tells them they can have whatever they want—all they have to do is ask. But Proverbs 16:3 says that when you trust God to do what *He* wants with your work, then things work out well.

The Christian life isn't about doing what you want. It is cooperating with God to do what both you and God want. How does that work? The closer you get to Him, the more you want to do what He wants.

What work do you have to do today? Is it homework or chores after school? Trust your work to the Lord by asking Him to help you with it. He will take it from there.

As I do my work today, Lord, I will ask You to help me. Teach me how to trust You better. I know that when I trust You, my plans will work out well.

154

SEEK GOD

"First of all, look for the holy nation of God. Be right with Him. All these other things will be given to you also."
MATTHEW 6:33

God made you to dream big dreams and make bold plans. But before you start making that list, God wants to do something in your life that may change your dreams and plans. It might make those dreams seem small when you compare them to God's bigger and bolder ideas.

That first thing you should do is *look for God.* Be right with Him by confessing your sins to Him. As you do so, He will give you "all these other things." What does that include? Earlier in the chapter, Jesus explained that He was talking about food, drinks, and clothing (Matthew 6:25). When you put this all together, Jesus wants you to seek God, confess your sins, and leave your basic needs to Him.

- -

I often think about what I want, God. I might ask You for some of those things. Help me to discover what would please You and then do what I know You want me to do.

155

TROUBLE COMES

[Jesus said,] "In the world you will have much trouble.
But take hope! I have power over the world!"
JOHN 16:33

You've probably gotten in trouble for something you did. If you lie to your parents or get into a fight at school or take something that isn't yours, there's a consequence. You may be punished and lose trust with the people you care about.

But you can also find trouble in things you *don't* do. Other people might say things that hurt you. Poor decisions by classmates or teachers or national leaders can affect you. Bad things will happen. God's Word promised that.

Sometimes, you make trouble. Other times, trouble finds you. Either way, God says He'll win. He's bigger than the bad stuff, so trust Him. Give Him your hopes and dreams, your successes and failures. He can make good out of anything.

* * *

When trouble comes—even if I create it—
help me, Father. Take my troubles and
do whatever You want with them.

DON'T WAIT

The Lord said to Abram, "Leave your country, your family and your father's house, and go to the land that I will show you."
GENESIS 12:1

You're much younger than Abram was in Genesis 12. In fact, he was older than most retired people today. In all those years, he'd lived in the same area with family members he knew and loved. He probably thought he would live there for his entire life. But God had other plans and told Abram it was time to move on. After he obeyed, God gave Abram a son, plus a lot of land and livestock. Abram's life proves that God can change anybody's future.

At some point in life, you'll sense that God is leading you to do something you didn't expect. Obey Him. Don't wait, even if it's hard. God has big plans for you when you obey Him.

· ·

When I obey you, Lord, I shouldn't be surprised when my new story is amazing. Give me the courage to obey, even when it's hard.

RICH AND FULL

Let the teaching of Christ and His words keep on living in you. These make your lives rich and full of wisdom. Keep on teaching and helping each other.
COLOSSIANS 3:16

Everyone has hopes and dreams. Most everyone wants to see things get better, not worse.

Dreaming of better things may be scary. Why? Because you don't know what it will take to get to a better place. Things might get worse before they get better. You might think it's easier just to stay where you are, doing things the way you've always done them.

But God says His plans never fail. So let Him help create *your* plans. Learn His Word. Talk about it with other people. The things God teaches make life rich and full. His plans make your dreams better. It makes them possible. It makes them good.

. . . .

Thank You for Your Word, Lord. I look forward to meeting with You every day as I read the Bible and learn how Jesus said to live.

HOPE IN THE RUINS

[God said,] "I will pay you back for the years that your food was eaten by the flying locust, the jumping locust, the destroying locust, and the chewing locust."

JOEL 2:25

The crops of God's people had been destroyed by locusts. If you have never seen one, they are like grasshoppers with big appetites. When there are a lot of them, farmers see their crops disappear fast. Locusts can leave fields empty with no food to eat or sell. But God told His people that if they would turn away from their sin, He would send them new grain, wine, and oil (Joel 2:19).

Do you ever feel like you've lost something? Maybe you've done something wrong, or maybe someone else has caused trouble for you. Know what? God is able to pay you back. That is no problem for Him. Don't focus on what you lost. Just keep your eyes on Jesus and watch Him work.

. . . .

Lord, I never want to complain about what I've lost. Instead, I want to focus on You, knowing You can pay me back for what I've lost.

ALL FOR NOTHING

Unless the Lord builds the house, its builders work for nothing. Unless the Lord watches over the city, the men who watch over it stay awake for nothing.
PSALM 127:1

If you make plans without God, then you are responsible for making your own dreams come true. But as a Christian boy who wants to become a man, that isn't a good idea. You will end up second-guessing your decisions and not asking for help until it's too late. And Psalm 127:1 says you can do all this work "for nothing."

If God isn't involved in your plans, then failure starts the moment you begin. God is big enough to protect your dream and complete your vision. But you have to trust Him, even when you can't see what He's doing. Besides, why would you want to spend all your time and effort on a plan that won't work?

I've been guilty of making plans by myself, Lord. I need to remember that You never promise to make my dreams come true, but You always invite me to dream together—with You.

LONG-RANGE PLANNING

Listen! You who say, "Today or tomorrow we will go to this city and stay a year and make money." You do not know about tomorrow. What is your life? It is like fog. You see it and soon it is gone. What you should say is, "If the Lord wants us to, we will live and do this or that."
JAMES 4:13–15

Adults sometimes talk about something called "long-range planning." This is an attempt to predict what they will be doing next year, five years from now, or even ten years in the future. They look at what they're currently doing and think about what they want to do later. Then they make choices they believe will help them get to the place they have planned for themselves.

The Bible talks about this and says there's a better way to plan. This plan is just fourteen words long: "If the Lord wants us to, we will live and do this or that."

You have given a good way for me to plan, God. Help me to be wise enough to remember that You have a plan that's far more important than what I think.

PLANS DELIVERED

When they had gone, an angel of the Lord came to Joseph in a dream. He said, "Get up. Take the young Child and His mother to the country of Egypt. Go as fast as you can! Stay there until you hear from Me."

MATTHEW 2:13

Jesus was born in Bethlehem. Mary and Joseph stayed there for months. One day, they were visited by wise men from the east. These men gave Jesus gifts. They experienced joy in meeting Him. When they left, Mary and Joseph may have wanted to think about the visit. Joseph, a carpenter, could have been thinking about ways to improve his business. God had other plans.

An angel came and said it was time to leave. He told them they would need to start their journey quickly. They were told their new home would be in Egypt. This wasn't their plan, but they changed their plans when they knew what God wanted. You can do that too.

. . . .

I read what You say in the Bible, Father. Help me be brave enough to change my plans if I learn that what I'm doing is not what You want me to do.

FAITH PLANS

Now faith is being sure we will get what we hope for. It is being sure of what we cannot see.
HEBREWS 11:1

Your plans and dreams will require faith. Words that have been used to describe faith are *trust, belief,* and *hope.* Hebrews 11:1 describes faith as something you believe will happen—even before it happens. Faith allows you to be certain God can do all the things you haven't seen yet—because His plans are always better.

The plans you make on your own always have the potential to make you sad. The plans God makes are always successful. Believing in God's plans means you win even before the plan is finished.

For a Christian, planning has always been about working *with* God to see a good outcome. It's never been about trying to do everything on your own. God is the only one who knows how things turn out. The best you can do is imagine.

- -

Your plans always succeed, Lord.
Help me trust Your plan and refuse to walk
forward with any plan but Yours.

WHEN THERE'S NO SHEPHERD

The false gods say what is not true. Those who use
their secret ways tell lies about the false dreams
they have seen. Their comfort means nothing.
So the people go from place to place like sheep and
are troubled because they have no shepherd.
ZECHARIAH 10:2

People can say things that sound true but aren't. And if you choose to believe their lies, then you can make plans based on bad information. What does that look like? Today's verse says it looks like sheep that wander away and get into trouble because they've chosen not to follow their shepherd.

In the Bible, Jesus is called the Good Shepherd. That means He's absolutely worth following. He'll always tell the truth and lead you right. And Jesus speaks to you through His Word, the Bible.

If anyone tells you something that disagrees with the Bible, the right choice is to believe your Good Shepherd. When you stray away from Him, bad things follow.

Don't let me be confused by lies, Lord.
Teach me to recognize truth and seek
Your wisdom in everything I do.

ASKED. ANSWERED.

The Lord came to Solomon in a special dream in Gibeon during the night. God said, "Ask what you wish Me to give you."
1 KINGS 3:5

What if God were to give you a gift of anything you wanted? This would be a dream come true. What would you ask for? Would it be the strength of a superhero, the skills of a star athlete, or just a new gaming system?

God offered Solomon that gift—he could ask for whatever he wanted, and God would give it to him. This was very unusual. What if Solomon, Israel's next king, had asked for something God had forbidden? But God knew what Solomon would choose. Perhaps that's why He made the offer. Solomon asked for wisdom to know how to lead God's people. It was a request that was easy for God to grant. The choice pleased Him.

You're encouraged to ask for wisdom, too, and God's Word says He'll give it to you (see James 1:5).

I ask because You said You would answer this prayer, Father. Give me wisdom to know You, follow You, and live for You.

GOOD PLANS INCLUDE...

"Wherever your riches are,
your heart will be there also."
MATTHEW 6:21

Some things that you value today won't be worth much in a garage sale two years from now. They're still worth having. But you should look for more important things that will keep their value much longer.

When you dream your dreams and make plans for your life, you should stop and think: Do they include things that last forever? Or will you grow tired of them and want to quickly move on to other things?

In Matthew 6, you're told to think about "your riches." Are they things that break, rust, and get stolen? Or are they things that last forever? When you ask God to help with your plans, make sure they mean something to more than just you.

. . . .

Where is my treasure, Lord? Show me if I have
chosen well or if I need to pursue better things.

WHEN MOUNTAINS MOVE

[Jesus said,] "If you have faith as a mustard seed, you will say to this mountain, 'Move from here to over there,' and it would move over."

MATTHEW 17:20

You've read about faith and how it's needed in the life of anyone who follows God. You need to believe God without doubting that He is who He said He is. You must hope in the future as you follow Him.

Jesus gave an example of those who accept God and believe without doubting. Jesus said this faith is a mountain-moving faith. God chooses to trust those who trust Him. He doesn't let them do whatever they want. Faith helps people do what *God* wants. And the results are miraculous.

What you do in faith isn't supposed to show how important you are but how important God is. When mountains move, God is working to do something you can't do on your own.

. . . .

If I could move mountains by myself, Lord, it would be easy to think I'm a hero. But I don't want to take the credit. I want to make sure people know You are the one who is good.

A PLAN TO HONOR

*Whatever you say or do, do it in the name
of the Lord Jesus. Give thanks to God
the Father through the Lord Jesus.*
COLOSSIANS 3:17

Your hopes and dreams are important to you. And they should be. These dreams are personal, and they involve a lot of thought and planning. God doesn't ever want you to think your dreams are unimportant, but He also doesn't want to see you fail. God's ways are absolutely the best ways, so if you want to experience the best, make sure every plan, hope, and dream for your future is something that honors Him.

By saying, "Whatever you do," this verse means, "If you have plans, dreams, and hopes—honor God with them." Before you make any moves, large or small, remember that the honor you give God will always help you discover His best plan.

*Help me to believe Your plans are worth
finding, Father. I want to know You, follow
You, and make my plans with You.*

FEAR-BEATING PROMISE

"Do not fear, for I am with you. Do not be afraid, for I am your God. I will give you strength, and for sure I will help you. Yes, I will hold you up with My right hand that is right and good."

ISAIAH 41:10

Fear is the great stop sign. It's colorful, multi-sided, and sharp-edged. It wants you to stop trying, stop believing, and stop dreaming. And fear wants you to hold onto it like it's a security blanket. But God's promise in today's verse is a reminder that you never need to.

When you're afraid, be encouraged by Isaiah 41:10. God made a very good promise that He continues to keep today. His promise is to give you strength, to help you, and to carry you through every situation. It's a fear-beating promise. Why? Because He loves you.

. . . .

Keep me from fear, Lord. Remind me that I'm helped and strengthened by You alone. And remind me that nothing that people can do to me is worth fearing.

FOLLOW YOUR LEADER

*The steps of a good man are led by the
Lord. And He is happy in his way.*
PSALM 37:23

Have you ever gone fishing or taken a hike or learned some new skill with an adult who loves you? They had to teach you a lot—what to do, what *not* to do, and how to stay safe. At first, it isn't easy to do a new thing in a new place. But as you watched and listened to your older, wiser teacher, it became easier—because you were following a good lead.

This is what your Christian life should look like. God shows you how to live as a Christian. You read His Word and then you begin to practice what you've learned. It isn't always easy at first, but as you continue to study and ask for guidance, you realize God created you to follow Him just like this.

Let me be the kind of student You want me to be, God. Show me, teach me, tell me, and watch me. I want to get things right—with Your help.

DROP IT OFF

[Jesus said,] "Come to Me, all of you who work and have heavy loads. I will give you rest."
MATTHEW 11:28

You have a job to do. But it's an easy one: bring all the stuff that feels like it's too much to deal with and give it to Jesus. You don't have to try harder and keep carrying it. You don't have to keep feeling like you are overloaded.

Jesus made a promise to those who are overwhelmed. When you bring all the struggle, trouble, and burden to Him, His promise is, "I will give you rest." He didn't say He would give you a pep talk and send you home. He didn't say that all you really needed to do was toughen up. If you've been struggling, then the only wise choice you can make is to pray. Tell Jesus all about it, and give Him your heavy load.

* *

Some things are just too much, Lord. I don't want to feel this way. You say I don't have to. Please take my burden. I can't seem to do anything with it.

A PROMISE KEPT

*[Moses said,] "The Lord will fight for you.
All you have to do is keep still."*
EXODUS 14:14

The Red Sea lay in front of hundreds of thousands of Israelites. An enemy army was behind them. They were trapped. At least that's what they thought. But Moses delivered a promise from God. The people just needed to calm down because God would take care of it. The sea did something no one had ever seen before—it split in two. Something like a road showed up on the sea floor. Then all the people walked between the walls of water to get to the other side.

God still does things like that today. You don't need to worry when God is taking care of you. You might not even know when He's done something that made a hard situation easier. But know that He is always there, always working for you. Hold on to the promise that the Lord will fight for you.

*Lord, You don't want me to respond to bad
things with anything other than trust in
You—the God who fights for me.*

STRENGTH TO THE WEAK

He gives strength to the weak. And He gives
power to him who has little strength.
ISAIAH 40:29

If you're feeling powerless, God wants you to turn to Him for strength. God pays attention. He knows when people are drained of energy. He knows when people want to give up. He even knows when they do. Yet He still promises to give strength to the weak and power to those with little strength.

God doesn't force you to take His help, though. In fact, He waits for you to ask. He is not being selfish. He just wants you to ask when you realize you can't do things on your own. That's when you will notice Him and the help that only He can bring to your struggle.

- -

Your promises make me wonder why I wait
so long to ask for help, God. When I'm weak,
because I will be, stand with me and give me
the strength I don't have without You.

A GOOD-NEWS REPORT

The Lord came to us from far away, saying, "I have loved you with a love that lasts forever. So I have helped you come to Me with loving-kindness."

JEREMIAH 31:3

If you ever watch the news, you'll see and hear about disasters that happen all over the world. It could be a volcano, a wildfire, or a hurricane. These news reports, sad as they are, can be a good reminder to pray for the people involved.

With all the bad news in our world, you might believe everything is falling apart and that no one can stop it. But Jeremiah 31:3 is a "news report" that should make you feel better. This news is a promise that changes everything. God said, "I have loved you with a love that lasts forever. So I have helped you come to Me with loving-kindness."

No bad news can overcome the good news of God's love.

- -

Heavenly Father, Your love is bigger than tornado and more powerful than an earthquake. I choose to trust You.

FORGIVEN AND HEALED

"If My people who are called by My name put away their pride and pray, and look for My face, and turn from their sinful ways, then I will hear from heaven. I will forgive their sin, and will heal their land."

2 CHRONICLES 7:14

God forgives you when you admit you're wrong for not following His rules. 2 Chronicles 7:14 is a good look at this promise.

When God said these words, Solomon had just finished building the temple. Because God knew the people of Israel would do the wrong thing over and over, He gave them the promise in today's verse. He wanted them to know He was for them and not against them, even when they sinned.

You can read these same words today, knowing that forgiveness is waiting when you break God's rules. Just turn your back on sin, admit you're wrong, and accept God's promised forgiveness.

- -

Today, I'm turning toward You, Lord. I admit I've been wrong. With Your help, I'll make a good choice. Today, I choose forgiveness. I choose You.

A GREATER GIFT

*Those who are right with the Lord cry, and He hears
them. And He takes them from all their troubles.*
PSALM 34:17

What is the saddest thing that ever happened to you? Did
your best friend move away? Or did one of your grandparents pass away? Or did you have to have a surgery? At
first, you didn't know how to react or what to think, right?
But when something bad happens, you can pray. The Old
Testament refers to this as crying out to God.

When you struggle, one of the best gifts anyone can
give you is his time to listen. Listening may be a greater gift
than helping. Everyone wants to be heard, and God says
He will not only hear what you have to say but He'll help.
That's His promise. So go ahead—cry out to Him today.

*Trouble keeps finding me, so God
I'm crying out to You today. Keep me close
and keep me safe. I need Your help.*

A FOREVER COMPANION

[Jesus said] "If you love Me, you will do what I say. Then I will ask My Father and He will give you another Helper. He will be with you forever."

JOHN 14:15–16

God promised more than His friendship—and that's an incredible promise. He also promised a helper. That helper is the Holy Spirit who teaches, encourages, and counsels you. And don't think He just drops by from time to time to see how you're doing. Jesus said, "He will be with you forever."

God doesn't make the gift of His Spirit available to those who don't love Him, to people who don't do what He says. This promise is for those who follow Christ. Jesus made that clear when He said, "If you love Me, you will do what I say."

You were created to love and obey Jesus, and His Spirit helps you do that.

. . . .

Thank You for Your Spirit, Father. He helps me learn to do what You've always wanted me to do. I have always needed a friend like this.

GIFT OF GOD

*For by His loving-favor you have been saved
from the punishment of sin through faith. It is not
by anything you have done. It is a gift of God.
It is not given to you because you worked for it.
If you could work for it, you would be proud.*
EPHESIANS 2:8–9

When someone gives you a gift at Christmastime, you might feel like you are supposed to give that person a gift in return—even if you didn't plan to. It doesn't feel right otherwise, does it? Some people think that's how heaven works. We do a lot of good things for God, then hopefully, He will give us the gift of eternal life. But that's not what the Bible teaches.

God didn't rescue you from the punishment of sin because of anything you did. You didn't work for or earn your salvation. If you could earn it, you would be a proud person and would go around bragging to your friends about how good you are. Instead, it is a gift of God. That should inspire us as Christians to tell others how good *God* is.

*You did everything I needed to be rescued, Lord.
Wow—I meant that much to You. Thank You!*

HE'S FAITHFUL: YOU'RE SAFE

*The Lord is faithful. He will give you strength
and keep you safe from the devil.*
2 THESSALONIANS 3:3

When you face challenges that are bigger than you can handle, it's nice when an adult takes care of them for you. God also takes care of hard things for you. He even takes care of problems you never even know about. Sometimes you'll need to ask for God's help. Sometimes He helps before you even think about asking.

God is never taken by surprise. He knows more than you—way more. He protects you from things that He doesn't want in your life. Those are the things Satan wants for you, and they're always bad. But God promises to provide the strength you need to keep you safe from the enemy.

. . . .

*There's more to my life than I can see, God.
Thank You for doing things for me that I never even
know about. Thank You for loving me that much.*

MUD PUDDLES AND SHOWERS

"The man who is right with God is taken away from what is sinful, and goes where there is peace."
ISAIAH 57:1–2

When you were young, you might have played outside and jumped in a mud puddle. Boys will do that sometimes. Dirty water stained your clothes and touched your skin. Your parents might have quickly put you into a bathtub or shower to get clean again.

That's a good picture of what God does for you. If sin is like a mud puddle, then God takes you out of it when you ask Him to. He cleans you up. When He does, you have peace with Him. He does all the work.

Know God, do the right things, get clean, discover peace.

. . . .

I'm tired of jumping in puddles and making a mess, Father. I want to be right with You. I want You to help me, clean me, and give me the peace that only comes from knowing You.

DO WHAT IS WRITTEN

"This book of the Law must not leave your mouth. Think about it day and night, so you may be careful to do all that is written in it. Then all will go well with you. You will receive many good things."

JOSHUA 1:8

Some of God's promises are about what He does for you just because He loves you. Some promises are for those who are willing to obey Him first.

Would it make sense for God to reward bad behavior? Would it be helpful to give you everything you want when you won't follow God? Would it be a good idea to not show God that you love Him but then expect Him to do great things for you?

God offers great news in Joshua 1:8. Things will go well, and good things will come—but first, God's rules must be known and valued. You must think about what God says so you can do what He asks.

I can become satisfied when I listen to You, and then do what You want, Lord. You promise me that all will go well when I follow Your rules.

GOD HEARS US

We are sure that if we ask anything that
He wants us to have, He will hear us.
1 JOHN 5:14

Many would love for this verse to read, "We are sure that if we ask anything. . .He will hear us." That sounds like there is nothing you could ask for that He won't give. But you've paid attention, right? God doesn't give you everything you ask for—but if you ask for something He already wants to give you, then you'll have His attention.

How can you know what He wants? By reading the Bible. As you think about what the Bible says, day and night, then you will know what God wants for you. As you read the Bible, God renews your mind. And then "the things you do will be good and pleasing and perfect" (Romans 12:2).

The things that You want for me are the things I
should ask for, God. Help me to learn what those
things are so I can ask—and You can answer.

EXPERIENCE JESUS' JOY

[Jesus said] "If you obey My teaching, you will live in My love. In this way, I have obeyed My Father's teaching and live in His love. I have told you these things so My joy may be in you and your joy may be full."
JOHN 15:10–11

If today's scripture was a suitcase, there would be a lot to unpack. What's inside starts with God's love and ends with His joy.

You were made to exist in the love God has for you. You'll need to recognize His love and accept it through faith in Jesus. But you won't experience that love if you don't follow God's directions found in His Book. If that seems like it might be too hard, just remember that Jesus never asks you to do something He didn't do. He said that He obeyed God and that He lived in God's love.

This scripture isn't just a reminder that obedience is important. It's another one of God's promises. He promised His love, and He promised His joy.

- -

You have great promises for a young man like me, Father. I will obey You today and expect to receive Your joy to the full.

NO FEAR

God did not give us a spirit of fear. He gave us a spirit of power and of love and of a good mind.
2 TIMOTHY 1:7

If you ever feel fearful, worried, or anxious, God wants you to know that those feelings don't come from Him. When you became a Christian, the Holy Spirit came to live inside you, and He gave you a spirit of power, love, and a good mind.

That doesn't mean that Christian boys won't sometimes be afraid. When the worries of this world creep into your mind, Satan tries to make you forget that you have a spirit of power, love, and a good mind. But you don't have to listen to him. In fact, you should refuse to believe the devil. Instead, memorize 2 Timothy 1:7 and use it against him.

Lord, You did not give me a spirit of fear. Help me to remember today's verse so I can be prepared the next time I feel fearful.

CHRISTIAN HOPE

*Let us hold on to the hope we say we have
and not be changed. We can trust God
that He will do what He promised.*
HEBREWS 10:23

Christian hope is different than this world's hope. When unbelievers use the word, they are wishing for something to happen. When Christians use the word, they truly believe that what God said will happen. No matter how hard your life might get, the writer of today's verse wants you to remember to hold onto hope—because God *will* do what He promised.

The next two verses in Hebrews 10 tell you how to do this: "Let us help each other to love others and to do good. Let us not stay away from church meetings. Some people are doing this all the time. Comfort each other as you see the day of His return coming near."

There's something to hope for—seeing Jesus in person!

*Lord, as I spend time with other Christians,
I find true hope in Your promises. As Your second
coming draws near, help me to remind
others about the hope of the gospel.*

HIDDEN TREASURE

I have looked for You with all my heart.
Do not let me turn from Your Law.
PSALM 119:10

There's no one like you. There never has been. There never will be. You were made to be an adopted son of God. That's an incredible truth. Your job now is to continue searching the scriptures and drawing close to God. God never intended for you to try to live without Him. You need His help.

Remember how God said that King David was a man who was pleasing to Him in every way (1 Samuel 13:14)? Even a man like King David needed to pray a prayer like the one in today's verse. As he continued with that prayer, he told us about his secret weapon: "Your Word have I hid in my heart, that I may not sin against You" (Psalm 119:11).

Hide God's Word in your heart. It will make you strong. It will make you the *you* God wants you to be.

. . . .

I want to hide Your Word in my heart, Father,
so that I won't turn from Your Law.

SCRIPTURE INDEX

MORE ENCOURAGEMENT AND WISDOM FOR BRAVE BOYS LIKE YOU!

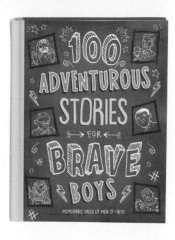

Boys are history-makers! And this compelling storybook proves it! This collection of 100 adventurous stories of Christian men—from the Bible, history, and today—will empower you to know and understand how men of great character have made an impact in the world and how much smaller our faith (and the biblical record) would be without them.

Hardback / 978-1-64352-356-9